DEFEAT AT GALLIPOLI:
THE DARDANELLES PART II, 1915–16

∘⊶⊰✣⊱⊷∘

uncovered editions

Series editor: Tim Coates

Other titles in the series

uncovered editions

DEFEAT AT GALLIPOLI

THE DARDANELLES COMMISSION

PART II, 1915–16

∾◦⊷⧓⊶◦∾

London: The Stationery Office

© The Stationery Office 2000

Applications for reproduction should be made in writing to
The Stationery Office Limited, St Crispins, Duke Street,
Norwich NR3 1PD.

ISBN 0 11 702455 4

First published as Cmd 371, 1918
© Crown copyright

A CIP catalogue record for this book is available from the
British Library.

Cover photograph © Imperial War Museum (Q13560):
Commodore Keyes, Vice-Admiral de Robeck, General Sir Ian
Hamilton and Major-General Braithwaite on board the *Triad*.
Used with permission of the Trustees of the Imperial War
Museum.

Typeset by J&L Composition Ltd, Filey, North Yorkshire.

Printed in the United Kingdom for The Stationery Office by
Biddles Limited, Guildford, Surrey.
TJ1160   C30   09/00

Uncovered Editions are historic official papers which have not previously been available in a popular form. The series has been created directly from the archive of The Stationery Office in London, and the books have been chosen for the quality of their story-telling. Some subjects are familiar, but others are less well known. Each is a moment of history.

Series editor: Tim Coates

Tim Coates studied at University College, Oxford and at the University of Stirling. After working in the theatre for a number of years, he took up bookselling and became managing director, firstly of Sherratt and Hughes bookshops, and then of Waterstone's. He is known for his support for foreign literature, particularly from the Czech Republic. The idea for 'Uncovered Editions' came while searching through the bookshelves of his late father-in-law, Air Commodore Patrick Cave OBE. He is married to Bridget Cave, has two sons, and lives in London.

Tim Coates welcomes views and ideas on the Uncovered Editions series. He can be e-mailed at timcoatesbooks@yahoo.com

In 1915, in response to a request from the Tsar of Russia to open a war front in the eastern Mediterranean, the British and their allies mounted an attack on the Gallipoli Peninsula in western Turkey.

The Gallipoli Peninsula lies on the European side of the Dardanelles, the narrow waterway which forms the main shipping route to the ports of southern Russia. Consequently it is of vital military and economic significance.

The Turkish Empire at that time was in alliance with Germany. However eager some British politicians were to respond to the request, the use of ground forces posed great problems, as the British Army was already heavily engaged in France. Recruitment was well short of the levels of any of the other great powers.

The attack was initially a naval assault on the fortresses guarding the southern entrance to the straits. It ended in failure, as reported in the sister volume in this series, Lord Kitchener and Winston Churchill: the Dardanelles Part I, 1914–15.

A fear of loss of face prompted the military commanders to gather a huge international force from all over the British Empire and to mount an ambitious land campaign without proper planning and without proper reconnaissance of the terrain. The enemy were already forewarned of the impending attack and were well prepared. The humiliating defeat which ensued and the huge losses incurred after only a few months of the campaign became the subject of a public inquiry. This book is the final part of that inquiry.

The realisation of the incompetence of the government's handling of this whole affair was instrumental in the formation of a coalition to replace the Liberal government, the removal of Winston Churchill as head of the Admiralty, and eventually the appointment of David Lloyd George as Prime Minister, instead of Herbert Asquith, in December 1916.

The Dardanelles (context map)

THE ORIGIN AND INCEPTION OF THE JOINT NAVAL AND MILITARY ATTACK

When the naval attack [on the Dardanelles] was sanctioned by the War Council on January 28th, 1915, there was no question of supporting it with large military forces. Such forces were not then available, and Lord Kitchener represented that they would not be available for some considerable time.

The Gallipoli Peninsula, 1915

MAP OF THE
GALLIPOLI PENINSULA

Scale 1:250,000

5 4 3 2 1 0   5   10 Miles

N

Sea Of Marmora

Baila Burnu (C Xeros)

Bulair

Gallipoli Straits

GALLIPOLI

GALLIPOLI
PENINSULA

Suvla Bay

S
E
L
L
E
N
A
D
R
A
D

CHANAK

The Narrows

Cape Helles

Kum Kale

Imbros

During January, 1915, the War Council were occupied in discussing their future military policy, based on the possibility of a stalemate in the Western theatre of war, and on the necessity of operations elsewhere.

In the course of these discussions, Lord Kitchener, on January 8th, expressed an opinion in favour of an attack on the Dardanelles. He then informed the Council that the Dardanelles appeared to be the most suitable military objective, as an attack there could be made in co-operation with the Fleet. He estimated that 150,000 men would be sufficient for the capture of the Dardanelles, but reserved his final opinion until a close study had been made.

These discussions resulted in two general conclusions.

The first conclusion was expressed in a despatch from Lord Kitchener to Sir John French on January 9th, in which Lord Kitchener wrote with regard to the possibility of the employment of British forces in a different theatre of war.

> The Council considered carefully your remarks on this subject in reply to Lord Kitchener's letter, and came to the conclusion that, certainly for the present, the main theatre of operations for British forces should be alongside the French Army, and that this should continue as long as France was liable to successful invasion and required armed support. It was also realised that should the offensive operations subsequently drive the Germans out of France and back to Germany, British troops should assist in such

operations. It was thought that after another failure by Germany to force the lines of defence held by the French Army and yours, the military situation in France and Flanders might conceivably develop into one of stalemate, in which it would be impossible for German forces to break through into France, while at the same time the German defences would be impassable for offensive movements of the Allies without great loss of life and expenditure of more ammunition than could be provided. In these circumstances it was considered desirable to find some other theatre where such obstructions to advance would be less pronounced, and from where operations against the enemy might lead to more decisive results.

For these reasons the War Council decided that certain of the possible projects for pressing the war in other theatres should be carefully studied during the next few weeks, so that as soon as the new forces are fit for action plans may be ready to meet any eventuality that may be then deemed expedient, either from a political point of view or to enable our forces to act with the best advantage in concert with the troops of other nations throwing in their lot with the Allies.

And the second conclusion was embodied in the decision recorded by the War Council on January 13th:

That if the position in the Western theatre of war becomes, in the spring, one of stalemate, British troops should be despatched to another theatre and objective, and that adequate investigation and preparation should be undertaken with that purpose and that a sub-committee of the Committee of Imperial Defence be appointed to deal with this aspect of the question.

Lieutenant-Colonel Sir Maurice Hankey in his statement comments on the second conclusion as follows:

Although this conclusion does not mention the Dardanelles as an objective, and probably had little influence over the decision to use troops against the Dardanelles, which was forced on the Allies by pressure of circumstances, it is of some importance as an indication that, in the opinion of the War Council, troops might have to be employed in some theatre of war other than the Western Front. Even the early investigations which preceded this decision had shown—what those held subsequently were to confirm—that there were only two alternative theatres of war to the Western Front at that time in the region of feasibility, namely, the Dardanelles and Serbia.

On January 13th and 28th, 1915, the War Council decided to attempt to force the Dardanelles by means of the Navy alone. A joint naval and military operation was not considered in consequence of Lord Kitchener's statement, accepted by the War Council, that there were not, and would not for some months be, any troops available for such an operation. At a meeting of the War Council on May 14th, Mr Churchill stated that if he had known three months before that an army of from 80,000 to 100,000 men would be available in May for an attack on the Dardanelles, the attack by the Navy alone would never have been undertaken.

Towards the end of January, diplomatic efforts were made to secure the co-operation of Greece with Serbia, which met with no success. As by February 15th the negotiations to secure Greek co-operation with Serbia had failed, attention began once more to be directed to the Dardanelles, and on February 16th the War Council decided to send the 29th Division, and a force from Egypt, to Lemnos to support the naval attack. It was also decided that the Admiralty should build special transports and lighters [large open boats used for loading and unloading ships], suitable for the conveyance of a force of 50,000 men and their landing at any point where they might be required. The despatch of the 29th Division was after-wards postponed till March 10th. The transports collected for this Division were countermanded by a message, delivered to the Director of Transports by Colonel Fitzgerald on behalf of Lord Kitchener. It is right, however, to say that the Director of Transports did not act on these instructions until he had orders to do so given to him by Lord Fisher, who was then First Sea Lord.

Future military plans were discussed in a series of meetings of the War Council on February 19th, 24th and 26th. At these meetings there arose an acute difference of opinion as to whether the 29th Division should be sent at once to the Eastern Mediterranean, and Lord Kitchener's anxiety about a possible German offensive on the Western Front caused him to withhold his consent to the despatch of that Division until March 10th.

From the record of these discussions it appears that the policy contemplated was:

(a) To support the naval attack with three divisions which Lord Kitchener thought might be required to secure the passage of the Straits after the fall of the forts.

(b) To concentrate as large a military force as possible in the Eastern Mediterranean ready to secure control of the Sea of Marmora, the Bosphorus, and Constantinople, after the Straits had been forced by the Fleet.

(c) As an alternative, to hold these forces ready for any action which might determine the attitude of the Balkan States, and thus bring into the struggle at least Romania and Greece, possibly Bulgaria, and unite the whole of the south-east of Europe with Britain and France in a combined action against the Central Powers.

In the course of these discussions, Lord Kitchener informed the Council "that if the Fleet could not get through the Straits unaided, the Army ought to see the business through. The effect of a defeat in the

Orient would be very serious. There could be no going back." The naval attack on the Dardanelles had committed us to offensive action in the Near East. The same view was expressed by Sir E. Grey, who stated that failure would be equivalent to a great defeat on land. Mr Asquith also told us that from this time onward Lord Kitchener was determined that the Army should see the naval attack through.

At the War Council on February 19th, Mr Asquith read out extracts from a memorandum of the General Staff prepared on December 19th, 1906, for the Committee of Imperial Defence, which was afterwards circulated to the members of the Council, and in which the possibility of a combined attack, naval and military, upon the Dardanelles had been considered.

This memorandum pointed out that:

> When the question of despatching a military expeditionary force to the Gallipoli Peninsula comes to be passed in review, the first point to be considered is the general one of whether a landing is possible at all, in face of active opposition under modern conditions.
>
> In regard to this, history affords no guide. The whole conditions of war have been revolutionised since such an operation was last attempted. Military opinion, however, will certainly lean strongly to the view that no landing could nowadays be effected in the presence of an enemy, unless the co-operating naval squadron was in a position to guarantee, with

its guns, that the men, horses, and vehicles of the landing force should reach the shore unmolested, and that they should find, after disembarkation, a sufficiently extended area, free from hostile fire, to enable them to form up for battle on suitable ground.

In the opinion of the General Staff, a doubt exists as to whether the co-operating fleet would be able to give this absolute guarantee.

The successful conclusion of a military operation against the Gallipoli Peninsula must hinge, as already stated, upon the ability of the fleet, not only to dominate the Turkish defences with gunfire, and to crush their field troops during that period of helplessness which exists while an army is in actual process of disembarkation, but also to cover the advance of troops once ashore, until they could gain a firm foothold, and establish themselves upon the high ground in rear of the coast defences of the Dardanelles.

However brilliant as a combination of war, and however fruitful in its consequences such an operation would be, were it crowned with success, the General Staff, in view of the risks involved, are not prepared to recommend its being attempted.

The Director of Naval Intelligence, while generally in agreement with the General Staff, and fully concurring as to the great risks involved in a joint naval and military enterprise against the Gallipoli Peninsula, expressed the view that:

The memorandum somewhat underrates the value of the assistance which might be rendered by a co-operating fleet by means of a heavy covering fire at the actual point of disembarkation and during the stages of the advance, immediately succeeding the landing, as well as by feints [distraction tactics] and diversions along the 45 nautical miles of littoral between the Bulair line and Cape Helles.

The effectiveness of covering fire from men of war, as an adjunct to land forces, was well illustrated by the Japanese attack on Kinchow, where the fire of the Japanese gun-boats turned the scale at the critical moment, and enabled the attackers to force the left of the Russian position, while the torpedo boats, in rear of the Russian lines, interrupted, by their fire, the passage of trains in either direction.

In that enterprise, the co-operating vessels were very small, and the fire they were able to develop was insignificant, compared with what might be brought to bear in the Gallipoli Peninsula, where the hydrographical conditions are such that any number of vessels of the largest size and power could be employed to support the land forces.

Sir Maurice Hankey informed us that it was generally held by the War Council that the General Staff memorandum of 1906 was not wholly applicable to the conditions obtaining in 1915. There is no record of the precise reasons for this opinion, but speaking from memory he thinks that they were somewhat as follows:

(i)   Turkey in the Balkan wars had shown herself to be much less formidable as a military power than had been previously assumed.

(ii) There had been a considerable development of naval ordnance since 1906.

(iii) The fall of the Liège and Namur forts led to the conclusion that permanent works could easily be dealt with by modern long-range guns.

(iv) By the use of aircraft the value of naval bombardment, especially by indirect laying, would be enormously increased.

(v)   The development of submarines led to the hope that the Turkish communications to the Gallipoli Peninsula through the Sea of Marmora would be very vulnerable.

On February 24th, the question of the appointment of a military commander was mentioned at the War Council, and the first to be considered was Lieutenant-General Sir William Birdwood. The scope of the military operations, however, gradually became enlarged, and it was thought advisable to select an officer of greater experience and higher rank. General Sir Ian Hamilton was appointed on March 12th, and sailed on the next day.

Following the decisions of the War Council, Lord Kitchener gave orders on February 20th for two Australasian divisions in Egypt to prepare for service at the Dardanelles; and by the end of February a French Division and the Royal Naval Division were ready to embark for the same destination. All these were placed under the command of Sir William Birdwood.

On February 23rd, Sir William Birdwood was ordered to proceed to the Dardanelles to confer with Admiral Carden. He then made a reconnaissance of the position and the telegrams which subsequently passed between him and Lord Kitchener show:

(a) That Lord Kitchener still intended troops to be used for minor operations only;

(b) That Sir William Birdwood, on the other hand, did not expect the Navy to force the Straits unaided; and

(c) That Sir William Birdwood fully appreciated the formidable character of the defences of the Peninsula, and anticipated that large military operations would be necessary.

In the course of these preparations Lieutenant-General Sir John Maxwell, Commander-in-Chief in Egypt, telegraphed to Lord Kitchener on February 24th that he understood that the Gallipoli Peninsula was everywhere heavily fortified and prepared for defence, and was practically a fort, advance against which from any quarter without heavy guns would seem to be hazardous. Sir John Maxwell was also impressed by the views of Colonel Maucorps, who was a member of the French military mission in Egypt, and who had been for five years the military attaché at Constantinople. On February 26th he telegraphed to Lord Kitchener an appreciation by

Colonel Maucorps, which recommended an attack on the Asiatic side of the Peninsula as presenting the least difficulties, and expressed the opinion that it would be extremely hazardous to land on the Gallipoli Peninsula, as the Peninsula was very strongly fortified for defence. It was also pointed out that the garrison of the Peninsula was 30,000 strong, composed of the 9th Division of the IIIrd Army Corps, with reserve formations, under the command of Djevad Pasha, who was an excellent and very energetic officer; and that the Bulair lines had been re-made and re-armed.

The object of the operations at the Dardanelles was to gain an entrance to the Sea of Marmora and dominate Constantinople. At a meeting on March 10th Lord Kitchener announced to the War Council that the "approximate strength of the forces available against Constantinople" would be 128,700 (see table).

Naval Division	11,000
Australasian Infantry	30,600
Australasian Mounted Troops	3,500
29th Division	18,000
French Division	18,000
Russian Army Corps	47,600
Total	128,700

It should be noted that the despatch of the Russian Corps referred to in the table was to follow and be contingent upon our obtaining access to

Constantinople through the Dardanelles and the Sea of Marmora.

The facts which have been mentioned show that from an early date in February a military landing on some scale on the Gallipoli Peninsula was contemplated, and that, as time went on, a landing in considerable force became increasingly probable. There was therefore sufficient time for a preliminary plan of operations and plan of landing to be put forward by the General Staff. Such would be the usual course. In fact, among the duties assigned to the department of the Chief of the Imperial General Staff in the King's Regulations is the preparation of plans of offensive operations and of plans of concentration and reinforcement in connection therewith. When asked by the Prime Minister at the War Council meeting of March 19th whether any general plan and scheme of disembarkation had been worked out, Lord Kitchener said that, though the question had been examined in the War Office, sufficient information was not forthcoming for the preparation of a detailed scheme of landing, which would be undertaken by Sir Ian Hamilton in concert with the Naval Commander-in-Chief. No general plan of operations had been prepared by the War Office. We can see no reason why a general plan or alternative general plans should not have been worked out, and we think that the elaboration of such a plan or plans by competent officers of the General Staff would have put the military problem in a clearer light before the War Council.

While the concentration of troops in the Eastern Mediterranean was proceeding, Admiral Sir Henry Jackson, who was writing frequent appreciations of the position in regard to naval action, presented a minute to Mr Winston Churchill on March 11th, in which he stated:

> The position has considerably changed recently; there are now ample military forces ready at short notice for co-operation with him [i.e. the Admiral], and I suggest the time has arrived to make use of them.
>
> To advance further with a rush over unswept mine-fields, and in waters commanded at short range by heavy guns, howitzers,* and torpedo-tubes, must involve serious losses in ships and men, and *will not* achieve the object of making the Straits a safe water-way for the transports. The Gallipoli Peninsula must be cleared of the enemy's artillery before this is achieved, and its occupation is a practical necessity before the Straits are safe for the passage of troops as far as the Sea of Marmora.
>
> I suggest the Vice-Admiral be asked if he considers the time has now arrived to make use of military forces to occupy the Gallipoli Peninsula, and clear away the enemy artillery on that side—an operation he would support with his squadrons.
>
> With the Peninsula in our possession, the concealed batteries on the Asiatic side, which are less formidable, could be dealt with more easily from the

---

* A short gun used for shelling at a steep angle; used in trench warfare.

heights on shore than by ships' guns afloat, and the troops should be of great assistance in the demolition of the fortress's guns.

Mr Churchill communicated this minute to Lord Kitchener, and asked him for a "formal statement of the War Office view as to land operations." To which Lord Kitchener replied on March 13th:

Most Secret.
In answer to your questions, unless it is found that our estimate of the Ottoman strength on the Gallipoli Peninsula is exaggerated, and the position on the Kilid Bahr Plateau less strong than anticipated, no operations on a large scale should be attempted until the 29th Division has arrived and is ready to take part in what is likely to prove a difficult undertaking, in which severe fighting must be anticipated.

On March 12th, Sir Ian Hamilton was appointed to command the Mediterranean Expeditionary Force, and was summoned to the War Office to receive his instructions from Lord Kitchener. In his evidence Sir Ian Hamilton told us that he made full notes of this interview shortly afterwards, and that Lord Kitchener informed him:

That I knew his feelings as to the value of the Near East. He said, rifle for rifle, at that moment he had made up his mind we could nowhere make as good use of the 29th Division as by sending them to the Dardanelles. With good luck each of its 12,000 rifles might attract 100 more to our side of the war.

But the diversion of this Division had been opposed.

I must clearly understand (1) that the 29th Division was only a loan, to be returned the moment they could be spared. (2) That every man, gun, rifle, or cartridge sent out to me is looked upon as sheer waste by powerful interests, both those at home and in France, who have strategical ideas.

He said we soldiers were clearly to understand that we were string number 2. The sailors said they could force the Dardanelles on their own, and we were not to chip in unless the Admiral definitely chucked up the sponge.

Once we started fighting we had to see the enterprise right through at all costs. No Asiatic adventure was to be countenanced.

Lord Kitchener then explained, at some length, that owing to our command of the sea, military operations on the peninsula itself would be a limited liability ... meaning thereby that the area was restricted, and as the numbers of the enemy would be restricted, so the numbers which would have to be drawn from home would be restricted. His idea was once we began to march about Asia Minor the liability would become unlimited, and I would very likely have to make demands on him for reinforcements of all descriptions, which in the present state of affairs would be very difficult to give.

The only information which Sir Ian Hamilton was able to obtain before leaving consisted of the official handbooks; the outline of a plan which had been worked out by the Greek General Staff for an attack on the Dardanelles; and a statement by Lord Kitchener that the Kilid Bahr Plateau had been entrenched and would be sufficiently held by the Turks, and that south of Achi Baba the point of the peninsula would be so swept by the guns of the fleet that no enemy positions would be encountered in that quarter. This last statement was made on the authority of a map which afterwards proved inaccurate, and of little use. From Sir Ian Hamilton's evidence it would seem that no really good maps were available until some were taken from Turkish prisoners.

He was not supplied with the memorandum, prepared by the General Staff in 1906, for the consideration of the Committee of Imperial Defence, together with the remarks of the Director of Naval Intelligence thereon, in which the possibility of a joint naval and military attack upon the Dardanelles was fully discussed; nor were the views of Colonel Maucorps, late French Military Attaché at Constantinople, reported by Sir J. Maxwell to Lord Kitchener on February 26th, communicated to him.

Sir Ian Hamilton was also informed that Major-General Braithwaite was to be his Chief of the

General Staff. General Braithwaite himself had been informed of his appointment on the afternoon of March 11th, and told to get a staff together. This he proceeded to do, and he also obtained such information as was available at the War Office, which was of a very meagre description.

On March 13th Sir Ian Hamilton again saw Lord Kitchener, and was given formal written instructions for his guidance.

These instructions were as follows:

1. The Fleet has undertaken to force the passage of the Dardanelles. The employment of military forces on any large scale for land operations, at this juncture, is only contemplated in the event of the Fleet failing to get through after every effort has been exhausted.
2. Before any serious undertaking is carried out in the Gallipoli Peninsula, all the British military forces detailed for the expedition should be assembled so that their full weight can be thrown in.
3. Having entered on the project of forcing the Straits, there can be no idea of abandoning the scheme. It will require time, patience, and methodical plans of co-operation between the naval and military commanders. The essential point is to avoid a check [repulse], which will jeopardise our chances of strategical and political success.
4. This does not preclude the probability of minor operations being engaged upon, to clear areas occupied by the Turks with guns annoying the Fleet, or for the demolition of forts already silenced by the

Fleet. But such minor operations should be as much
as possible restricted to the forces necessary to
achieve the object in view, and should as far as practicable not entail permanent occupation of positions
on the Gallipoli Peninsula.

5. Owing to the lack of any definite information we
presume that the Gallipoli Peninsula is held in
strength, and that the Kilid Bahr Plateau has been
fortified and armed for a determined resistance. In
fact we must presuppose that the Turks have taken
every measure for the defence of the Plateau, which
is the key to the Western Front at the Narrows, until
such time as reconnaissance has proved otherwise.

6. Under present conditions it seems undesirable to
land any permanent garrison, or hold any lines on
the Gallipoli Peninsula. Probably an entrenched force
will be required to retain the Turkish forces on the
Peninsula and prevent reinforcements arriving at
Bulair, and this force would naturally be supported
on both flanks by gun-fire from the Fleet. Troops
employed on the minor operations mentioned above
(paragraph 4), should be withdrawn as soon as their
mission is fulfilled.

7. In order not to reduce forces advancing on
Constantinople, the security of the Dardanelles pas-
sage, once it has been forced, is a matter for the
Fleet, except as in paragraph 6 with regard to Bulair.
The occupation of the Asiatic side, by military forces,
is to be strongly deprecated [argued against].

8. When the advance through the Sea of Marmora is
undertaken, and the Turkish fleet has been destroyed,

the opening of the Bosphorus, for the passage of Russian forces, will be proceeded with. During this period, the employment of the British and French troops, which will probably have been brought up to the neighbourhood of Constantinople, should be conducted with caution. As soon as the Russian Corps has joined up with our troops, combined plans of operations against the Turkish army (if it still remains in European Turkey) will be undertaken, with a view to obtaining its defeat or surrender. Until this is achieved, landing in the town of Constantinople, which may entail street fighting, should be avoided.

9. As it is impossible now to foretell what action the Turkish military authorities may decide upon, as regards holding their European territories, the plan of operations for the landing of the troops and their employment must be left for subsequent decision. It is, however, important that as soon as possible after the arrival of the Fleet at Constantinople, all communications from the West to the East across the Bosphorus, including the telegraph cables, should be stopped. Assuming that the main portion of the Turkish army is prepared to defend European Turkish territory, it may be necessary to land parties to hold entrenched positions on the East side of the Bosphorus, and thus assist the Fleet in preventing all communication across the Bosphorus.

10. Should the Turkish army have retired to the East side of the Bosphorus, the occupation of Constantinople and the Western territories of Turkey may be proceeded with.

11. As in certain contingencies, it may be important to be able to withdraw our troops from this theatre at an early date, the Allied troops working in conjunction with us should be placed in those positions which need to be garrisoned, and our troops might, with advantage, be employed principally in holding the railway line, until a definite decision is come to as to future operations.

12. You will send all communications to the Secretary of State for War, and keep him fully informed of the operations and your anticipations as to future developments.

March 13th, 1915   KITCHENER

Sir Ian Hamilton, General Braithwaite, and the General Staff left on March 13th, arriving at Mudros [in Lemnos] on the 17th.

The administrative branches of the Staff did not start until a later date, arriving at Alexandria on April 1st.

Immediately on his arrival Sir Ian Hamilton attended a conference with Vice-Admiral Sir John de Robeck on board the *Queen Elizabeth*. This conference was attended by Admiral de Robeck, Sir Ian Hamilton, Général d'Amade, Admiral Guepratté, Admiral Wemyss, General Braithwaite, Commodore Keyes and Captain Pollen.

Sir Ian Hamilton told us that in the course of this conference he was informed by Sir John de Robeck that:

The Peninsula is rapidly being fortified, and thousands of Turks work like beavers all night on trenches, redoubts, and entanglements.

Not one living soul has yet been seen, but each morning brings evidence of nocturnal activity. All landing places are now commanded by lines of trenches, and are effectively ranged by field guns and howitzers, which so far cannot be located, even approximately, as our naval seaplanes are too heavy to rise out of rifle range.

He said the Turkish searchlights were fixed and mobile, they were of the latest pattern, and were run by skilled observers. The Germans evidently got hold of the Turks, and all that sort of work was being done in shipshape style by the Turks ...

The War Office had taken too sanguine a view in thinking that the ships' guns would be able to prevent the Turkish troops lodging themselves on the Peninsula, because de Robeck said he knew they were there from seeing the trench work increased every morning.

Many more troops have come down. The German officers have grappled with the situation, and have got their troops scientifically disposed, and heavily entrenched. So much so that they have not much to fear from the flat-trajectory guns of the Navy. The number of field guns on the Peninsula is now many times greater than it was.

On March 18th the substance of this conference, except as regards the small effect likely to be produced by the flat-trajectory gun-fire of the Navy, was telegraphed by Sir Ian Hamilton to Lord Kitchener.

And in a private letter, Sir Ian Hamilton, on the same day, wrote to Lord Kitchener:

> Here, at present, Gallipoli looks a much tougher nut to crack than it did over the map in your office.
>
> The increases to the garrison, the new lines of trenches, nightly being excavated, the number of concealed field guns, the rapidity of the current, are all brought forward when discussing military operations.
>
> My present impression is that, if it eventually becomes necessary to take the Gallipoli Peninsula by a military force, we shall have to proceed bit by bit.

It may here be noted that on May 9th Sir John de Robeck telegraphed to the Admiralty:

> The Navy has not been able to give the Army as great assistance as was anticipated. The Navy is of small assistance when it is a matter of trenches and machine guns, and the check of the Army is due to these factors.

On March 19th the failure of the naval attack on the previous day was discussed at a meeting of the War Council, and Mr Churchill was authorised to inform Sir John de Robeck that he could continue the naval operations if he thought fit. In the course of the discussion which followed, Sir Maurice Hankey's notes show that Lord Kitchener said he had given Sir

Ian Hamilton as many men as he could use on the ground.

On March 18th Sir Ian Hamilton made a reconnaissance down the coast, arriving at Cape Helles to find the naval engagement in "full blast."

On the 19th the result of this reconnaissance was communicated by him to Lord Kitchener in the following telegram, which was received *after* the War Council mentioned in the last paragraph:

> Yesterday we steamed close along the western shore of the Gallipoli Peninsula. Here and there landing places were, of course, observed.
>
> So near were we that we could see quite clearly the barbed wire defences covering the trenches ...
>
> I have not yet received any report of the naval action, but from what I actually saw of the extraordinary gallant attempt made yesterday, I am being most reluctantly driven towards the conclusion that the Dardanelles are less likely to be forced by battleships than at one time seemed probable, and that if the Army is to participate, its operations will not assume the subsidiary form anticipated.
>
> The Army's share will not be a case of landing parties, for the destruction of forts, etc., but rather a case of a deliberate and progressive military operation, carried out in order to make good the passage of the Navy.

This telegram had been despatched at 2 pm. At 5.45 pm on the same day the following reply was sent by Lord Kitchener:

With reference to the last paragraph of your telegram of today. You know my views that the passage of the Dardanelles must be forced, and that if large military operations on the Gallipoli Peninsula by the Army are necessary to clear the way, they must be undertaken, after careful consideration of the local defences, and must be carried through.

On March 20th Sir Ian Hamilton intimated to Lord Kitchener that "he understood his views completely."

On March 22nd Sir Ian Hamilton had another conference with Sir John de Robeck on board the *Queen Elizabeth*. This conference was attended by Admiral de Robeck, Sir Ian Hamilton, Admiral Wemyss, General Braithwaite, General Birdwood, and Captain Pollen.

Sir Ian Hamilton's note of this conference is to the following effect:

He [i.e. Vice-Admiral de Robeck] is now quite clear and strong that he cannot get through without the help of all my troops.

Wemyss agreed with de Robeck.

No voice was raised to question the momentous decision.

The result of this important conference was then communicated by Sir Ian Hamilton to Lord Kitchener, and by Sir John de Robeck to Mr Churchill, in the following telegrams:

(1) Sir Ian Hamilton to Lord Kitchener, March 23rd:

I have now conferred with the Admiral, and we are equally convinced that to enable the Fleet effectively to force the passage of the Dardanelles, the co-operation of the whole military force will be necessary.

The strength of the enemy on the Gallipoli Peninsula is estimated at about 40,000, with a reserve of 30,000 somewhere west of Rodosto.

The unsettled weather prevailing in March introduces a dangerous, incalculable factor into the operation of landing a large force in face of certain opposition, but the weather next month should be more settled, and I am sanguine of the success then of a simple, straightforward scheme, based on your broad principles.

I have already worked out the main features of my scheme, and I can communicate them, if you think it safe to do so.

Practically the whole of my force will be required to effect what I have planned, and on the thoroughness with which I can make the preliminary arrangements, of which the proper allocation of troops, etc., is not the least important, the success of my plans will largely depend.

This is one of the principal reasons why I attach importance to the thorough organisation of the expedition at a convenient base like Alexandria.

(2) Sir John de Robeck to First Lord [Mr Churchill], March 23rd:

At a meeting today with Generals Birdwood and Hamilton, was informed by the latter that the Army will not be ready to commence military operations until the 14th April.

All guns of position guarding the Straits must be destroyed, in order to keep up our communications when the Fleet gets through the Sea of Marmora. These guns are numerous, and not more than a small proportion of them can be put out of action by gun-fire.

The enemy were obviously surprised by the landing of a demolition party on the 26th February.

Judging by the events of the 4th March, future operations of this nature will probably meet strenuous and well-considered opposition.

It does not appear to me practicable to land a sufficient force inside the Dardanelles to carry out this service. This view is shared by General Hamilton.

On the other hand failure to destroy the guns may well nullify any success of the Fleet, by enabling the Straits to be closed up, after the ships have gone through, and there may not then be ships available to keep the Straits open, as losses may be heavy.

Until the Sea of Marmora is reached, the mine menace, which is much greater than we expected, will remain. This requires careful and thorough treatment, both in respect of mines and floating mines.

Time will be required for this, but arrangements can be made by the time the Army will be ready.

A decisive operation about the middle of next month appears to me better than to take great risks for what may well be only half measures.

It now appears to me that there may, possibly, be above the Narrows, mine-fields of which we have very little information.

Obstacles may be sunk in the Channel by the Germans, and submerged hulks and pontoons placed there. I have in mind particularly the very large pontoons in the Golden Horn, on which the old Road Bridge from Stambul to Pera was laid.

The howitzers, which it is so difficult to spot from the sea, will, of course, remain.

I think it will be necessary to take and occupy the Gallipoli Peninsula by land forces before it will be possible for first-rate ships, capable of dealing with the *Goeben* [German battlecruiser] to be certain of getting through, and for colliers [coal-bearing boats] and other vessels, upon which the usefulness of the big ships largely depends, to get through.

(3) Sir John de Robeck to First Lord [Mr Churchill], March 26th:

The check on the 18th March is not, in my opinion, decisive, but on the 22nd March I met General Hamilton, and heard his views, and I now think that to obtain important results, and to achieve the object of the campaign, a combined operation will be essential ...

For the Fleet to attack the Narrows now would jeopardise the success of a better and bigger scheme and would, therefore, be a mistake.

(4) Sir John de Robeck to First Lord [Mr Churchill], March 27th:

On the 22nd after conference with the General and acquaintance with his views, I gathered that he considered co-operation of the Army and Navy to be a sound operation of war, and that he was quite prepared to co-operate with the Navy in forcing the Straits, although he could not take action until the 14th April.

In my opinion, decisive and overwhelming results will be effected by the plan discussed with General Hamilton, and now being prepared . . .

The assumption underlying the plan originally approved for forcing the Dardanelles, by ships, was that forts could be destroyed by gun-fire alone. As applied to the attacking of open forts, by high velocity fire, this assumption has been conclusively disproved.

For example, the damage caused to Fort 8 is, possibly, the disablement of one gun, though this fort has frequently been bombarded at long and close range. The destructive power of shells which hit, was either uselessly expended on the parapet, or only effected the demolition of some unimportant outwork in the background of the fort.

It has been impracticable, even at ranges of 700 or 800 yards, to obtain direct hits on each gun. This was attempted in the case of Forts 3 and 6. In Fort 4, on the 26th February, although the fort had been heavily shelled for 2 days, at both long and short range, one gun was found loaded and ready to fire. At the most it is possible for ships to dominate the forts to such an extent that the guns cannot be fought by their crews. To effect more permanent disablement would require an excessive expenditure of ammunition at point blank range.

This opinion is strengthened by recently received information on the operations against Tsin Tau. The analogy of the attack on the cupola forts at Antwerp by heavy howitzer fire is quite misleading, when applied to the case I have described.

It is necessary for ships to come under fire at the Narrows, in order to engage Forts 7 and 8 at close range. It is necessary, therefore, to silence these, and this entails expenditure of valuable ammunition. I am also in some anxiety as to the wear of the old guns. Several premature bursts of common shell occurred on the 18th and put guns out of action from time to time. A bombardment, which could not be carried to a decisive result, would be the worst policy. It is, therefore, necessary to land demolition parties to destroy forts.

General Hamilton is not prepared to undertake the task of covering these parties at the Narrows and I quite agree. It is impracticable to carry out the demolition by surprise. The difficulties of clearing a passage for the Fleet (and the forts have to be kept silenced by gun-fire, while it is carried out) are materially increased by the dangers from mines, which are greater than we anticipated, and the number of torpedo tubes, which are reported to have increased, and which cannot be destroyed.

I consider the result of naval action might be either a brilliant success or quite indecisive. A great factor towards success is the effect that would be produced on the Turkish Army by the appearance of the Fleet off Constantinople. The situation in Turkey, at present, appears to be controlled by the Army, but this in itself is dominated by the Germans.

If the advent of the Fleet into the Sea of Marmora fails to dismay the Turkish Army, and they close the Straits behind us, ships would only be able to operate and maintain themselves in the Marmora for a length of time that is governed almost entirely by the number of ammunition ships and colliers which can accompany them, and the percentage of unprotected ships which we can expect to get through is small, as the passage will be contested.

While the forts are still intact I can see no practical solution to the problem of passing supply ships for the Fleet through the Dardanelles. It would be vital, in this event, for the Peninsula to be occupied by the Army, as the guns on the Asiatic side can be commanded from the European shore, sufficiently to permit ships to pass through. This would open the Strait.

The assistance of all naval forces available will, in my judgment, be needed to land the Army of the size contemplated, in the teeth of strenuous opposition.

The Turks would not, necessarily, be induced to abandon the Peninsula by a landing at Bulair, and there is no doubt that this can better be done by a fleet intact outside the Straits than by the remnants of a fleet, short of ammunition, inside the Straits.

Our success would be assured when the Army holds the Peninsula and the squadron is through the Dardanelles.

Co-operation, which would really prove the deciding factor in reducing the length of time necessary for the completion of the campaign in the Sea of Marmora, and for the occupation of Constantinople, will be ensured by this delay of perhaps a fortnight.

These telegrams mark the close of the period of consultation between Sir Ian Hamilton and Sir John de Robeck as to the policy to be pursued. Thereafter these officers were occupied with detailed plans for the landing. It is only necessary to observe:

(*a*) That Sir John de Robeck's views, as expressed in his telegram of March 27th, were endorsed by Mr Churchill's telegram, in reply, of the same date:

That the result might have been achieved without involving the Army, according to the original plan, had been my hope, but I see clearly that a combined operation is now essential for the reasons you mention.

The date is not distant, for time has passed and the troops are available. The Admiralty telegram, approving all your proposals, will, therefore, be sent.

(*b*) That Sir Ian Hamilton's plan of operations was to some extent anticipated by Lord Kitchener in a telegram to him on April 2nd:

Limpus's report, which I have been reading, and of which the Admiral has a copy, seems to point to the advisability of effecting the main landing in the neighbourhood of Cape Helles and Morto Bay, while making a feint [diversion tactic] in considerable force south of Kaba Tepe, with the possibility of landing and of commanding the ground of Sari Bahr, so that the enemy, on its southern slopes, may be prevented from supporting those on the Kilid Bahr Plateau.

I presume that, preparatory to destroying the forts at the Narrows, you will attack in force to occupy this plateau. The most necessary points for consideration seem to me, at a distance, to be night attacks, and crossing barbed wire entanglements.

As to entanglements, which artillery fire has not completely cleared, it is worth remembering how thorn zaribas [barriers] were successfully crossed in the Sudan by means of the native angerib bed. Men carrying angeribs are placed immediately behind the hand grenade and attacking lines and directly the fire of the defence is dominated, they rush forward and place the angerib on the entanglement. A recrudescence [fresh break out] of fire from the trench may ensue, which is again dominated, and the process continued until men can jump over the last entanglement. If each attacking company does this, many roads over obstructions can be made.

I do not in the least wish to influence your judgment, formed locally, on the situation to be dealt with in the Gallipoli Peninsula, but only give you all this for what it is worth.

I hope that arrangements will be made for adequate bombardments by the Navy of the positions to be attacked, and for the advance of your troops to be covered by its shell fire. When you have decided on your plans, I shall be glad to have a general idea of them. Secrecy will be observed here.

To which Sir Ian Hamilton replied on April 4th:

Reference concluding sentence, there is no need to send you my general idea as you have already got it in one, even down to the details.

I have not got enough gun ammunition to destroy barbed wire by field guns, howitzers, or machine guns, and the entanglements are mostly defiladed [protected end-to-end] from naval guns. I therefore must rely on other methods, including that suggested by you.

After March 19th there was no further meeting of the War Council until May 14th, and we are unable to ascertain any precise date on which, after the failure of the naval attack, military operations on the

Gallipoli Peninsula were definitely decided on. Mr Asquith informed us that between these dates there were thirteen meetings of the Cabinet, at eleven of which the operations at the Dardanelles were brought up for report; and that they were on several occasions the subject, not merely of report, but of long and careful discussion.

It would appear therefore that these operations and the policy they involved were undertaken with the knowledge of the Cabinet, but we think, as was stated in our previous report, that they should have been fully discussed by the War Council.

During this period negotiations took place for the intervention of Italy on the side of the Allies; and the course of these negotiations made it undesirable to discontinue operations after the failure of the naval attack. Lord Kitchener had, as we have previously stated, told the War Council on February 24th that, if the Fleet could not get through the Straits unaided, the Army ought to see the business through. The same opinion was expressed in his written instructions to Sir Ian Hamilton on March 13th.

In addition, the failure to penetrate the German lines at the battle of Neuve Chapelle and in the Champagne (Perthes) had strengthened the view that a stalemate had set in in the West. The need for relieving the pressure in the Caucasus still existed. The urgency of opening up a line of communications, first to supply Russia with munitions and military stores, and secondly, to enable the Russian harvest of 1914 to be exported and thus re-establish the Russian exchanges, had not diminished. And undoubtedly the fear existed that to abandon the enterprise might have a bad effect in Russia.

These considerations, together with the fact that the military difficulties had not been sufficiently realised, seem to have led to the decision to initiate the joint naval and military attack on the Gallipoli Peninsula.

THE PREPARATIONS FOR THE LANDING

Sir Ian Hamilton's Administrative Staff did not arrive at Alexandria [in Egypt] until April 7th. The preparations for the landing were, therefore, carried out by his General Staff. With regard to these preparations it is necessary to consider:

(*a*) The change of the main base from Lemnos to Alexandria.

(*b*) The necessity for re-loading and re-arranging the transports of the 29th and the Royal Naval divisions, and

(*c*) The estimates made of the strength of the Turkish forces to be encountered.

CHANGE OF BASE FROM LEMNOS TO ALEXANDRIA

Lemnos had been originally selected as a base for the naval attack in February and March. Lemnos was also contemplated as the base when, on February 16th, the War Council decided to send out the 29th Division. On February 20th, 30,000 Australian troops under Sir William Birdwood were ordered by Lord Kitchener to get ready to lend further support to the naval attack, and a brigade of these troops was sent from Egypt to Lemnos, arriving there early in March. On February 23rd Vice-Admiral Sir Sackville Carden telegraphed to Sir John Maxwell that, before the landing on the Gallipoli Peninsula, the troops sent from Egypt would have to live on board their transports; and on February 26th he sent a similar message, adding that the troops could land for exercise.

On March 2nd, the War Office telegraphed to Sir William Birdwood:

> Reports from Athens indicate that there is no water at Mudros Bay. Special arrangements for distilling and for tank vessels are being made by the Admiralty, but there may be some delay.

After consulting the naval authorities on the spot, please report on the subject.

On March 9th the Royal Naval and the French Divisions began to arrive at Lemnos, and on that date Sir John Maxwell transmitted to the War Office a telegram from Admiral Carden to the effect that, since the water supply was not assured, no more troops should be sent from Egypt for the present. This was followed, on March 12th, by a further telegram transmitted from Admiral Wemyss, reporting that a water supply for 10,000 men and their horses was available, but that disembarkation was difficult and tedious with the appliances at their disposal, that embarkation would be still more difficult, and suggesting that troops coming from Egypt should be held in readiness there. On March 16th, Sir John Maxwell informed the War Office that "he gathered from Admiral Wemyss and the officers on the spot that Lemnos could not be a base for a large force." In addition to this, it was found necessary to repack the transports, and it was impossible to do this at Mudros. On March 18th Lord Kitchener sanctioned Alexandria as the main base, subject to the final decision of Sir Ian Hamilton and Sir John de Robeck.

Thereafter Alexandria was used as the main, and Lemnos as the advanced base.

THE RE-LOADING AND RE-ARRANGEMENT OF TRANSPORTS

The allocation of the transports for the 29th and Royal Naval Divisions was made by the War Office and by the Royal Marine Office of the Admiralty respectively. When the transports for the 29th Division arrived at Avonmouth, it was found that some of them had already been partially loaded at another port with fodder for horses, and it was accordingly impossible to stow on them all the vehicles forming the first line transport for the units on board. This part of the first line transport was sent on three freight ships which had been told off [detailed] to take the Mechanical Transport belonging to the Division, and these ships arrived ten days later than the transports.

In addition to this, some of the ships were not well or conveniently stowed.

The units of the Royal Naval Division, also, were not embarked complete, the personnel having been placed in one ship, the transport in another, and the horses in another. The stores were not packed as they should have been owing to their not having arrived until a few hours before the ships sailed.

Proposals were made to restow at Malta the transports which were bringing out the 29th Division, but the accommodation in the harbour did not permit this. The transports were, therefore, sent to Alexandria, and some delay was caused by the fact that they had to await the arrival of the slower ships (presumably the freight ships), which had essential things on board.

No special instructions were given in the first instance as to how the transports should be packed. The reason for this was that the exact use to be made of the troops was not decided, and no plan of operations had been prepared. The ordinary principles which govern embarkation in the absence of special instructions therefore applied. We were informed by the Director of Movements that these principles are:

(1) To split up units as little as possible.
(2) To ensure that, when units are split up, the ships on which they are embarked should sail on the same day, or on dates as near each other as possible.
(3) To embark troops in such a way that they should be able to take to the field at once on disembarkation.

He explained, however, that these principles cannot always be adhered to, especially in the matter of sending men and their transport together. Many transports, especially the larger ships, some of which were used in this instance, are not fitted to carry animals or vehicles. Transports are not collected at a port and then loaded simultaneously, but dealt with as they arrive. It is possible to carry units and their first line transport together if instructions are given to do so, but it takes a longer time and requires a larger number of transports, because in that case the transports would have to sail only partly loaded.

In this case no such special instructions were issued. It would have been hardly possible to do so, as the plan of operations was not determined. General Braithwaite, Sir Ian Hamilton's Chief of the General Staff, says that no one could have given the order satisfactorily unless he had worked it backwards from the shore on which he wished to disembark the men, and nothing of that kind was possible here. Indeed the plan was so little known that a great deal of transport which was quite useless for the actual expedition was taken, e.g. a much larger number of horses than was necessary, and all the mechanical transport required according to the ordinary war establishments [military forces]. The Quartermaster-General's department at the War Office pointed out that the mechanical transport would not be needed, but it was sent by the direct order of the Secretary of State. When the objects of the expedition became more clearly defined, this was discontinued.

We think therefore that, in the absence of a scheme of operations, a considerable amount of restowage would in any case have been necessary. The chief complaint made against the packing was the separation of the men from their first line transport and animals, and this has been explained above. There was some bad stevedoring [loading and unloading], but it must be remembered that at Liverpool, where part of the force embarked, there were considerable troubles as to dock labour; that this was the first long sea embarkation that had been undertaken by the officers in charge; and that the orders were suddenly given and had to be carried out at once.

On the whole we think that, though there may have been instances of bad stowage, the real reason for the extensive repacking was the absence of know-ledge of the operations for which the embarkation was required, and that the embarkation officers at the ports of loading were not to blame.

At first sight the delay caused by this repacking and the change of base from Lemnos to Egypt appears serious, but on examination we think that the effect was very slight. When the transports were ordered to Alexandria and Port Said to repack, no plan of operations had been settled, the whole of the Staff had not yet arrived, and there were many arrangements to be made. The first mention of repacking is on March 18th, 1915, and the last repacked transport left Alexandria on April 16th, 1915. The landing was on April 25th, 1915. We think that plans and arrangements could not have been completed until the greater part of this inter-val had elapsed, and that the effective delay did not amount to more than a few days, which was not important.

The Administrative Staff did not arrive in Alexandria until April 1st.

The Commander-in-Chief and General Staff left for Mudros shortly after, leaving the Administrative Staff behind. Major-General Woodward, the Deputy Adjutant-General, protested against this decision to the Commander-in-Chief and the Chief of the General Staff, but did not succeed in getting it reversed. We think that the Chiefs of the Administrative Staff should have accompanied General Headquarters, it being of high importance that these officials should be in touch with the Commander-in-Chief and work in close concert with the Chief of the General Staff.

ESTIMATE OF TURKISH FORCES

Before the landing Sir Ian Hamilton estimated the strength of the Turkish forces on the Gallipoli Peninsula as 40,000 with a reserve of 30,000 west of Rodosto. This estimate was increased, later, by the addition of the 2nd Army Corps Nizam, which had been moved in April from the Caucasus to Constantinople, and made available to reinforce the forces on the Peninsula.

A more detailed and comprehensive estimate was conveyed by the War Office in a telegram to the General Staff in India on March 1st:

> We appreciate the situation as follows:
>
> It is believed that divisions now consist of Nizam brought up to establishment by Redif.
>
> In European Turkey, including Gallipoli, are nine divisions, totalling 120,000 men.
>
> In Smyrna, Asiatic Dardanelles, and Panderma there are two strong divisions, and depot battalions, totalling 40,000 men.

In Caucasus there are 17 divisions, many of which are weak, totalling 190,000 men.

In Syria and Palestine there are five divisions, totalling 70,000 men.

In Mesopotamia is a 4th Division (new formation) of 1st Corps of 12 battalions, lately arrived Baghdad, also 35th and 38th divisions.

It is possible that the 6th Reserve Corps is also in the Caucasus, though its reported existence is not yet confirmed.

After the landing had been effected, Sir Ian Hamilton presented a revised estimate in his telegram to Lord Kitchener of April 30th:

The Turkish troops are as follows:

1. 2nd, 7th, 8th and 9th divisions, all of 3rd Army Corps; Pamir Division of 3rd Reserve Corps; part of 5th division, 2nd Army Corps. Total, say, 44,000.

2. Probably on Peninsula, but not definitely ascertained, 11th Division and part of 10th, both of 4th Army Corps, and perhaps 44th and 58th Regiments unallotted. Total, say, 26,000. This information has mainly been ascertained from statements by prisoners. Documents obtained locally and found on dead Turks show that two regiments have just come from Plagak.

3. Not on Peninsula, but available at short notice, part of 6th Army Corps. Say, 20,000.

Bulair is watched by the Fleet, and already three demonstrations have been made, but it is impossible to stop reinforcements crossing the Isthmus during the night.

Generally reinforcements arrive by the sea to Gallipoli, but as the fleet have now two submarines off that town, I hope this will be rendered very dangerous in future.

The Gallipoli Peninsula, 1915

5 4 3 2 1 0   5   10 Miles

Scale 1:250,000

N

Ejelmer Bay

GALLIPOLI PENINSULA

▲ Karakol Dagh

Suvla Burnu

Suvla Bay   Salt Lake   ● Anafarta Sagir

● Buyuk Anafarta

Beach Z (Anzac Cove)   ▲ Sari Bair

Hell Spit   ● Boghali

● Kojadere

▲ Kaba Tepe

● Eski Keui

● Maidos

S E L L E N A D D A R D

● Kilid Bahr   ● CHANAK

The Narrows

IMBROS

Beach Y   ● Achi Baba

Gurkha Bluff   ● Krithia

Beach X

Tekke Burnu Beach W   Beach S

Cape Helles   Morto Bay

Beach V   Sedd el Bahr

● Kum Kale

Kephez Burnu

THE LANDING ON APRIL 25TH

Two important questions to be considered concurrently in drawing up a plan of operations were the place or places of landing on the peninsula, and the objective or objectives of the troops when landed.

As regards the first of these questions, Sir Ian Hamilton had, when at Mudros, made such reconnaissance as could be made from the sea, and states that the dominating features in the southern part of the peninsula were:

(1) Sari Bahr mountain, 970 feet high.
(2) Kilid Bahr Plateau, 700 feet high, a natural forti-
    fication artificially fortified, covering the
    Narrows from an attack from the Aegean.
(3) Achi Baba, 600 feet high, commanding the
    extreme south of the peninsula near Cape Helles.

After considering the other plans open to him he
decided to make two main landings: one, which was
divided into several subordinate landings, in the
extreme south of the peninsula; and the other north
of Kaba Tepe and near the south-western foothills of
Sari Bahr.

In his despatch he mentions two other main
alternatives which he considered:

(1) A landing on the north coast of the Gulf of
    Xeros, and
(2) A landing on the Asiatic shore of the Dardanelles.

He rejected the first on the ground that Bulair
would lie between him and the Narrows, and that in
attacking Bulair he would be open to attack from the
Turkish forces in Thrace.

He had made a reconnaissance of Bulair, and had
come to the conclusion that it was not possible to
effect a landing there.

He did not think that he had a sufficient force for
operations on the Asiatic shore, and his instructions
from Lord Kitchener were opposed to a landing
there.

These are the only alternatives discussed in the despatch, but others were considered, and Suvla is mentioned in an appreciation signed by Colonel Aspinall and submitted to Sir Ian Hamilton's Chief of the General Staff. A landing there is dismissed in a few words, and it does not seem to have been thought to be a place which merited the same attention as Bulair and the Asiatic coast. Probably the reason for this was that when it was decided to land on the European side, but not to attempt a landing at or near Bulair, it was considered that the best way to help the Fleet was to attack at the southern end of the peninsula. This is the opinion expressed by Sir Ian Hamilton and by General Braithwaite.

The question also must have arisen whether the available force was sufficient for more than two main landings. In order to make Suvla Bay secure as a base it was necessary to occupy the northern ridge by the sea, the Karakol Dagh, up to Ejelmer Bay, and thence the heights running south from Ejelmer Bay to Anafarta Sagir. Sir Ian Hamilton did not consider that he had sufficient force to do this as well as land at Anzac and Helles, and Lieutenant-General Sir Aylmer Hunter-Weston also said that the force would not have been strong enough for such an operation.

Sir William Birdwood expressed the opinion that, looking at the matter in the light of after-events and assuming that there was no greater force defending Suvla at that time than at the later landing, Sir Ian Hamilton's force was sufficient to have landed at Suvla with safety, and that it would have been well to do so; but he added: "I also think I should have done what Sir Ian Hamilton had done, only in the light of what has happened since and the inability to force Achi Baba."

Sir Aylmer Hunter-Weston informed us that, once a landing had been decided upon, he thought Sir Ian Hamilton's choice of landing places was a perfectly justifiable one.

On the other hand, several witnesses criticised the selection of the landing places, and expressed themselves in favour of other schemes of disembarkation. Whatever weight may attach to these divergent opinions, we consider that the choice of landing places was a matter lying within the discretion of the General Officer Commanding-in-Chief, and Sir Ian Hamilton appears to us to have exercised his discretion with reasonable care and circumspection.

As regards the objective or objectives of the troops when landed, we gather from the instructions issued by General Braithwaite to the General Officers commanding the Australian and New Zealand Army Corps and the 29th Division respectively, and the latter's Operation Orders based on these instructions, that the following movements were contemplated.

At Anzac the force which landed first, called the covering force, after it had overcome any resistance at or near the shore which the Turks might offer, was to occupy the Sari Bahr heights and thus cover the left flank of the force, called the main body, which was to land shortly afterwards. This body was to advance four miles east of the landing-place and assault Mal Tepe, a hill overlooking the Straits and three-quarters of a mile south of Boghali.

At Helles the troops were similarly divided into a covering force and main body, and after overcoming any resistance at or near the shore which the Turks might offer, they were to occupy Krithia and Achi Baba.

When the Anzac and Helles forces had established themselves at Mal Tepe and Achi Baba, the intention was that a converging attack should be made from those points upon the Turkish position at Kilid Bahr.

As the Turkish resistance near the shore proved too strong at Anzac and Helles, the proposed advance inland to Sari Bahr, Mal Tepe, Krithia, and Achi Baba did not take place.

It has been already stated that there were several distinct landings at the extreme southern end of the peninsula, and this was the subject of considerable comment by several witnesses. Speaking generally, it is not wise to divide a force, as it is thereby exposed to the danger of being attacked and beaten in detail. Sir Ian Hamilton's reasons for doing so in this case are given in his despatch of May 20th, 1915, published in the *London Gazette* of July 6th, 1915,* where he says:

> Nothing but a thorough and systematic scheme for
> flinging the whole of the troops under my command

---

*Reproduced in *British Battles of World War I, 1914–15*, another volume in the *Uncovered Editions* series.

very rapidly ashore could be expected to meet with
success, whereas on the other hand, a tentative or
piecemeal programme was bound to lead to disaster . . .
The beaches were either too well defended by works
and guns or else so restricted by nature that it did not
seem possible, even by two or three simultaneous
landings, to pass the troops ashore quickly enough to
enable them to maintain themselves against the rapid
concentration and counter-attack which the enemy
was bound in such case to attempt. It became necessary,
therefore, not only to land simultaneously at as many
places as possible, but to threaten to land at other points
as well. The first of these necessities involved another
unavoidable if awkward contingency—the separation
by considerable intervals of the force.

In view of the restricted space on the beaches and the
importance of preventing a concentration of the
Turkish forces against the small numbers which could
be landed at any one place, we are not prepared to question the propriety of Sir Ian Hamilton's dispositions
[arrangements].

The landing places selected were S at the north-
east corner of Morto Bay, V and W (called Lancashire
landing) on each side of Cape Helles, X (called
Implacable landing) just above Tekke Burnu, and Y,
just above Gurkha Bluff, and due west of Krithia.
There was another beach called Y2, which was considered, but no landing was made there. What
afterwards was known as Anzac was Beach Z, a little
to the north of Kaba Tepe. The nature of the beaches

is fully described in Sir Ian Hamilton's despatch, to which reference has already been made, and the description need not be repeated. A landing was also made by the French at Kum Kale, on the Asiatic side, but this was only intended to be temporary, and these troops were soon withdrawn to a position on the right of the British forces at Helles.

The landings at V, W and X were intended to be the main landings, those at S and Y being intended mainly "to protect the flanks, to disseminate the forces of the enemy, and to interrupt the arrival of his rein-forcements."

A feint was also made in the neighbourhood of Enos in order to prevent Turkish troops from being sent from the north of the peninsula to resist the landings.

We propose to discuss the arrangements for the provision of water and the care of the sick and wounded in a separate part of this report, and it is not necessary therefore to refer to them here except to say that the landing operations at Helles and Anzac were not checked by a lack of water.

The landings, as described in Sir Ian Hamilton's despatch, appear to have been well planned, and were carried out in the face of exceptional difficulties and at the cost of heavier casualties than had been expected. The conduct of the forces engaged was exemplary.

An unfortunate sense of unfairness was created by the fact that when Sir John de Robeck's despatch dealing with these operations was published, the troops employed at certain landings were praised by name, whereas those who landed at Beach V, which was regarded as the most difficult of all to capture, were praised without identifying them. The explanation is that Sir John de Robeck's despatch, as written, contained a detail of the troops assigned to the several landings, and reference to this showed at once that the battalions whose successful accomplishment of their task at Beach V "bordered almost on the miraculous" were the 1st Royal Dublin Fusiliers, 1st Royal Munster Fusiliers, and 2nd Hampshire Regiment. But this detailed list was withheld from publication as likely to give useful information to the enemy, and the troops in question were inadvertently denied the public tribute of Sir John de Robeck's praise.

It is not necessary to discuss the landings except in the case of that on Beach Y, as to which there seems to have been some misunderstanding. The landing on this beach was made by the 1st King's Own Scottish Borderers, under Colonel Koe, and the Plymouth Battalion of the Royal Marine Light Infantry, under Colonel Matthews. Colonel Matthews, as the senior officer, was in command.

The object was to move inland and try to capture a gun which was stated to be in position there, and make a demonstration so as to draw the enemy in that direction, and relieve the pressure at the foot of the peninsula. The force was then to withdraw and work up towards Beach X to join the rest of the 87th Brigade, to which the Royal Marine Light Infantry were attached. The united force would then move on Krithia.

The landing was made without opposition, and 2,000 men were on the ridge in a very short time. They advanced in the direction ordered, but were not met by the force coming from Beach X, which was unable to make its advance as proposed. Colonel Matthews then withdrew to the head of the gully up which he had advanced, and entrenched there.

The force was undisturbed by the enemy until between 4 and 5 pm, when it was attacked by a large number of Turks coming from the direction of Krithia. After hard fighting extending over many hours, the force under Colonel Matthews, having suffered many casualties and exhausted practically all its ammunition, was obliged to retire to the beach and re-embark.

The decision to withdraw was made by Colonel Matthews.

Immediately after landing, he had reported that there was no opposition, and afterwards, when attacked by superior forces and in want of ammunition, had sent a message to say that unless he had more ammunition he must withdraw: but he did not receive an answer to either message.

If a larger force had been landed at this beach in the first instance, or if it had been possible, either by diverting some part of the troops from Beach X or otherwise, to send reinforcements before the Turkish troops came up in the evening, a further advance might have been made, but it is difficult to say whether, without the expected co-operation from Beach X, it would have been successful.

At Anzac the landing was effected after severe fighting at a place rather further north than was intended, and in the confusion of landing the tows crossed one another, and the battalions got mixed, which checked the advance and made delay for reorganisation necessary.

The fighting was so severe throughout April 25th and the ground gained so small that by the evening, Sir William Birdwood feared that it might be necessary to withdraw the troops and informed Sir Ian Hamilton accordingly.

In reply the latter directed him to maintain his position at all costs.

Both at Anzac and at the south of the peninsula the troops by the evening of the first day after the disembarkation were occupying positions on and near the shore. At the south, contact had been established across the extreme end of the peninsula. In neither case, however, was it found possible to carry the advance beyond a short distance from the shore.

At Anzac it had been intended to occupy Sari Bahr and Mal Tepe, and at Helles to occupy Krithia and Achi Baba, within a very short time of the first landing, and ultimately to have effected a junction of the Anzac–Helles forces. In both cases the difficulties proved too great to permit these intentions being carried out, and in fact none of these objectives was ever attained.

The nature of the ground was a formidable obstacle, but the main difficulty lay in the fact that the Turks had been warned of the probability of an attack by the bombardment of the forts, followed by the assembling of troops, and consequently had made preparations by trenches, wire entanglements, etc., protected by artillery, machine-guns and rifle fire, to resist the attack; that they were in considerable force and well led (partly by German officers); and that they fought extremely well both in defence and counter-attack.

An opinion had prevailed, in consequence of the events of the Balkan wars and some recent fighting in Mesopotamia, that the Turkish soldiers had deteriorated as fighting men, but the fighting at Helles and Anzac during the landing and in the following months proved this to be a mistaken view.

Heavy and continuous fighting, described in Sir Ian Hamilton's despatch, followed for several days, with the result that a little more ground was gained and the positions improved, but very little real progress was made. The force at Helles was reinforced during May by the arrival of the 29th Indian Brigade, the 42nd (Territorial) Division, and three Battalions of the Royal Naval Division. If the Indian Brigade and the 42nd Division had been assembled at Mudros and ready to support the attack of the 29th Division, Brigadier-General Street, senior General Staff Officer with Sir Aylmer Hunter-Weston, was of the opinion that the attack would have been successful.

Sir Aylmer Hunter-Weston was not so confident on this point.

The evidence does not make it clear why these troops were not sent at once, but if it were possible, looking to all the circumstances, to send them, we think it would have been well to do so. On the evidence before us we see no reason why they should not have been sent. Sir Ian Hamilton expressed a wish for the services of a brigade of Gurkhas, but we cannot find that he definitely applied for the troops mentioned above.

Throughout these attacks there was a shortage of artillery and gun ammunition.

We must again refer to Sir Ian Hamilton's despatch for the particulars of this fighting, but it may be useful to quote some of his telegrams. They express an optimistic opinion of the chances of ultimate success, but they do not disguise the difficulties.

On April 30th, 1915, he gave as an estimate of the Turkish forces in or about the peninsula:

(1) On the peninsula, 44,000.
(2) Probably on the peninsula, 26,000.
(3) Not on the peninsula, but available at short notice, 20,000.

On May 4th he reported that the supply of ammunition was becoming a serious matter owing to the continuous fighting, to which Lord Kitchener replied that the supply was not calculated on the basis of a prolonged occupation of the Gallipoli Peninsula, and said: "It is important to push on." On May 7th he reported that some progress, but not so much as he had hoped, had been made, and that progress was slow and opposition stubborn. On May

9th, after describing the third consecutive day's attack on Achi Baba, he said:

> I might represent the battle as a victory, but actually the result has been failure, as the main object remains unachieved. Our troops have done all that flesh and blood can do against semi-permanent works, and they are not able to carry them. More and more munitions will be needed to do it. I fear this is a very unpalatable conclusion, but I see no way out of it.

He then estimated the forces engaged in the following manner:

> I estimate that the Turks had about 40,000 opposed to our 25,000 rifles. There are 20,000 more in front of the Australian–New Zealand Army Corps, 12,000 rifles at Kaba Tepe. By bringing men over from the Asiatic side the Turks seem able to keep up their strength. I have only one more Brigade of the Lancashire Territorial Division to come, and that will not suffice to make any appreciable difference in the situation as regards pushing through.

To this Lord Kitchener replied that the whole situation naturally gave him some anxiety, particularly as the transport service was much hampered by the want of ships.

On May 10th, Sir Ian Hamilton reported that the guns of the Navy had not been able to give him so much help as he had hoped, because of the spoon-shaped nature of the ground from Achi Baba to Cape Helles, which exposed only the outer edges to direct fire, while the inner slopes consisted of broken ground facilitating concealed works.

He explained that the 25,000 rifles which he had mentioned the day before had been a reference to the number of British rifles actually in the fighting line. The telegram continues:

> With regard to future operations, the Admiral agrees with me in thinking that the only sound procedure is to hammer away until the enemy gets demoralised. Meanwhile grand attacks are impracticable and we must make short advances during the night and dig in for the day until we get Achi Baba. I then hope to be able to make progress without this trench method, but Achi Baba is really a fortress. If two fresh divisions organised as a corps could be spared me I could push on from this end and from Kaba Tepe with good prospects of success, otherwise I am afraid it will degenerate into trench warfare with its resultant slowness.

On May 11th, Lord Kitchener cabled that he was sending out the Lowland Division and some artillery, and this message was acknowledged on May 12th.

On May 13th, Sir Ian Hamilton telegraphed, expressing a hope that the 29th Division would be made up to strength by drafts.

It was the rule to send out 10 per cent of an expeditionary force to replace casualties in the first instance. At the time of this expedition the rule had fallen into abeyance in the case of units going to France, the distance being short and communication rapid. Although the troops for the Dardanelles were to operate at a distance from England, Lord Kitchener would not allow the additional 10 per cent to be sent with them. The matter was mentioned to him by Lieutenant-General Sir Henry Sclater, the Adjutant-General, to whom it had been represented by Brigadier-General Woodward, who was Director of Mobilization at the War Office at the time of his appointment as Deputy Adjutant-General of the Expeditionary Force. Sir Henry Sclater said the reason given to him by Lord Kitchener for his decision was that the operations in Gallipoli would so soon be over that to form a base in Egypt would be practically locking up men who were much more urgently required in France. In Sir Henry Sclater's opinion, the men could not have been sent without denuding France of reinforcements, but General Woodward dissented from this view.

THE DECISION TO CONTINUE
THE OPERATIONS

In these circumstances an important meeting of the
War Council was held on May 14th to discuss the
situation.

It was clear that the conditions had materially
changed. The landings had been successfully effected,
but the expectation that it would be possible to
carry the important positions of Achi Baba and Sari
Bahr in the first rush had definitely failed, the task

having proved far more difficult than was anticipated. The casualties had been very heavy; they
amounted to about 14,000, exclusive of the French.
This made the question of drafts and reinforcements
very serious. It was now apparent that the operations
would not follow the course which had been
expected. Instead of the troops on landing being able
rapidly to drive the Turks out of their positions and
to occupy the heights dominating the defences of
the Narrows, they found themselves confronted by
lines of entrenchments and entanglements, possession
of which could only be gained by the deliberate
methods of trench warfare.

Probably at this time the very large expenditure
of ammunition required to reduce hostile trenches
had not been thoroughly realised, but, as already
pointed out, Sir Ian Hamilton had informed Lord
Kitchener on May 9th, 1915, that more and more
munitions would be needed, and it was known that,
as afterwards stated on May 17th, 1915, the advance
could probably be made with half the loss of life then
reckoned upon if there were a liberal supply of gun
ammunition, especially of high explosive. The positions held by the force were unfavourable: they
consisted of hardly more than a fringe. They were,
including the beaches, commanded by shell-fire, and
there were no opportunities for withdrawing the
troops for rest behind the line. At Helles the positions
were exposed also to shell-fire from the Asiatic shore,
though this was afterwards kept down to a great
extent by the fire of monitors.

The problem of transport was serious. There was a scarcity of ships and, owing to the necessity of using Mudros as a subsidiary base for troops, munitions, and stores, this scarcity was aggravated. Mudros had practically none of the usual facilities of a port. Stores not immediately wanted had to be kept on board the transports. Communication with different ships and different parts of the harbour was much impeded by want of light craft. Besides, there was always the probability of danger from submarines. In consequence the transports were detained at Mudros, and great delay and congestion resulted.

This condition of Mudros as a port was probably not of much importance so long as the operations were expected to be of short duration, but it was a serious matter which had to be faced if the operations were materially prolonged in time and enlarged in extent.

The Dardanelles Expedition could not be considered by itself; though great results were expected from it if successful, it was subsidiary, in the view of the military authorities in England, to the main operations in France.

The demands from France for both men and munitions were very great, and there was much difficulty in supplying them. An offensive at Festubert, disappointing in its result, took place in May, and it was obvious that the demands of France were likely to increase rather than decrease. Moreover, there were requirements in Egypt, Mesopotamia, and elsewhere, which had to be met.

There was another matter which had to be considered. As stated in our interim report, the occurrence which led to action being taken with a view to forcing the passage of the Dardanelles was an enquiry from the Russian Government on January 2nd, 1915, as to whether the British Government could do anything to relieve the Turkish pressure upon their troops in the Caucasus. A reply was sent that a demonstration would be made in the direction of the Dardanelles; and when this demonstration took shape, it was arranged that in the event of our gaining access to the Sea of Marmora the Russians should co-operate with us, if possible, by sea and land in the vicinity of Constantinople.

A Russian Army Corps was designated for the purpose of military co-operation; but before the scheme, so far as Constantinople was concerned, had any chance of becoming operative, the Russian reverse in Galicia had begun, and it seemed possible that this occurrence, apart from its influence on the Balkan states, might lead to a diversion of the force which was to be available near Constantinople, should we succeed in forcing the passage of the Dardanelles.

On May 12th the Admiralty ordered the withdrawal of the *Queen Elizabeth* from the Dardanelles Expedition, this decision being strongly opposed by Lord Kitchener. It is difficult to say why Lord Kitchener should have attached so much importance to the retention of the *Queen Elizabeth*. Naval gun-fire in support of the military operations had not hitherto proved to be as valuable as had been anticipated, and the reduction in naval gun power entailed by the withdrawal of the warship in question was stated by the Admiralty to be more than made good by the addition of monitors and other vessels to the Fleet.

The War Council had to determine whether, in the changed circumstances, the requirements of all the different areas of war could be supplied, and whether it was wise to continue the operations on the peninsula. Diplomatic efforts had been made ever since the beginning of the Dardanelles Expedition to secure the co-operation of the Balkan states, the most prominent and powerful being Bulgaria, and these states were much influenced not only by the course of current events, but by their appreciation of the consequences likely to result from the action in the Near East which was being taken or contemplated by the Central Powers on the one hand and the Entente Allies on the other. It was important, therefore, not to do anything which would show weakness. The expedition had been begun in consequence of a communication from Russia, and the Russians considered that the effect so far had been to hold up Turkish troops and relieve the pressure on their forces. It was hoped that, if successful, the expedition would open the way to Constantinople.

Finally, it was anticipated that an abandonment of the expedition would have a very bad effect upon British prestige in the East.

All these matters were taken into consideration, as well as the purely military question of the prospects of success of the operations in which we were engaged.

The tendency was towards sending out sufficient reinforcements for a further effort, but no final decision was reached, except that Lord Kitchener should ask Sir Ian Hamilton what force he would require to ensure success at the Dardanelles.

As a result of this decision, Lord Kitchener telegraphed to Sir Ian Hamilton on May 14th:

> The War Council would like to know what force you consider would be necessary to carry through the operations on which you are engaged. You should base this estimate on the supposition that I have adequate forces to place at your disposal.

On May 17th, Sir Ian Hamilton answered, pointing out the difficulties of the position, and concluded:

> If the present condition of affairs were changed by the entry into the struggle of Bulgaria or Greece or by the landing of the Russians, my present force kept up to strength by the necessary drafts, plus the Army Corps asked for on May 10th, would probably suffice to finish my task. If, however, the present situation continues unchanged, and the Turks are still able to devote so much exclusive attention to us, I shall want an additional Army Corps, i.e., two Army Corps additional in all. I could not land these reinforcements on the peninsula until I can advance another 1,000 yards, and so free the beaches from the

shelling to which they are subjected on the western
side, and gain more space, but I could land them on
the adjacent islands of Tenedos, Imbros and Lemnos,
and take them over later to the peninsula for battle.
This plan would surmount the difficulties of water
and space on the peninsula, and would perhaps
enable me to effect a surprise with the fresh
divisions. I believe I could advance with half the loss
of life that is now reckoned upon if I had a liberal
supply of gun ammunition, especially of high
explosive.

Lord Kitchener, on May 18th, replied, expressing
his disappointment that his preconceived views as to
the conquest of positions necessary to support the
troops on land were miscalculated, and his opinion
that the question of whether we could long support
two fields of operations draining on our resources,
required grave consideration. He concluded:

> I know that I can rely on you to bring the present
> unfortunate state of affairs in the Dardanelles to as
> early a conclusion as possible, so that any
> consideration of a withdrawal, with all its dangers in
> the East, may be prevented from entering the field of
> possible solutions.

Sir Ian Hamilton's telegram of May 17th afforded
the information called for by the War Council on
May 14th, and would, no doubt, have been considered at once, but, unfortunately, just at this time the

political crisis which resulted in the formation of the Coalition Government took place, and no authoritative conclusion was arrived at until June 7th.

Between these two dates the War Council had been increased in numbers by the addition of some members of the Unionist Party, and its name had been changed to that of the Dardanelles Committee. Its members were Mr Asquith, Lord Lansdowne, Lord Curzon, Lord Grey, Lord Crewe, Lord Kitchener, Lord Selborne, Mr Lloyd George, Mr Bonar Law, Mr McKenna, Mr Balfour and Mr Winston Churchill. Sir Edward Carson became a member in August, after the Suvla operations.

In Mr Churchill's opinion this political crisis produced an unfortunate delay by preventing an "unbroken and uninterrupted stream of reinforcements." According to his evidence Lord Kitchener, before May 14th, had informed him that it was intended to send two divisions. Therefore Mr Churchill had provided the transport for them, and informed Sir Ian Hamilton of the fact, but after May 14th Lord Kitchener changed his mind and sent one division only. At the same time Sir Ian Hamilton's telegram of May 17th was held over till after the formation of the new Government, and no action was taken on it. Mr Asquith agrees that the political situation was the main cause of the delay in sending reinforcements, but thinks that there was a shortage of available troops. Lieutenant-General Sir John Cowans also says that there was a difficulty in getting and equipping the men. We think that the political crisis was the main cause of delay. The Government had to decide whether operations other and larger than were originally contemplated should be undertaken. This was a question of policy, and some of the new members of the Government had to be satisfied that the expedition was a justifiable enterprise.

On May 28th, Lord Kitchener prepared a memorandum for the use of the members of the Dardanelles Committee, describing the objects and progress of the operations up to that date, and setting out what he considered to be the different courses then open. This appreciation shows that the difficulties which had been experienced by Sir Ian Hamilton had been communicated to Lord Kitchener, and that they were brought by him to the distinct notice of the members of the Committee.

In this document he pointed out that

> the difficulties of the enterprise had proved more formidable than was at first anticipated, and that a much greater effort than was originally budgeted for was now required.

After describing the course of events, he repeated:

> The main advantage of withdrawing from the Dardanelles is to put an end to an operation the difficulties of which have been underestimated, which has already made a considerable inroad on our resources, and which will make a very considerable

drain on both our naval and military resources before it is brought to a successful conclusion.

He then discussed the advantages of withdrawal, and summarised his conclusions as follows:

Three solutions offer themselves:
(1) Withdrawal
(2) To seek, if possible, an immediate decision
(3) To continue to push on and make such progress as is possible.

The disadvantages of withdrawal have been shown above to be so great that this course could, in my opinion, only be justified in order to avoid a great disaster.

On the other hand, it has been shown that the military forces and, what is even more important, the necessary supplies of ammunition asked for by the General Officer Commanding on the spot cannot be spared to bring the affair to a rapid conclusion, though I am somewhat in doubt, from the experience of trench warfare in Flanders, whether such increased forces would enable him to carry the position as he anticipates. Sir John French's forces have been increased very greatly, but no such advance as he had anticipated has occurred.

The third course, however, has much to commend it. It avoids any immediate blow to our prestige; it keeps the door open to Balkan intervention; it ensures our hold on a strategical position of great importance, which rivets the attention of the Turks and in all probability limits active operations on their part against Egypt, or in Mesopotamia, or the Caucasus.

The only thing to be said against it is that it involves certain dangers, viz., the risk arising from German submarines and of gas, assisted by the prevailing north winds. There are furthermore, in my opinion, possibilities of the Turks not being able to maintain resistance on the present scale. This would enable our troops to advance, as well as to take advantage of any movement that Bulgaria or Greece may take in our favour.

On June 2nd, Sir Ian Hamilton had telegraphed to the effect that, in his opinion, the change in the Russian military position owing to reverses in Galicia had set free 100,000 Turks; that there were 80,000 in the peninsula; and that he might have, in all, a quarter of a million men brought against him. He concluded:

Taking all these facts into consideration, it would seem that for an early success some equivalent to the suspended Russian co-operation is vitally necessary. It is, broadly, my view that we must obtain the support of a fresh ally in this theatre, or else that there should be got ready British reinforcements to the full extent mentioned in my telegram of May 17th, though, as stated above, the disappearance of Russian co-operation was not contemplated in my estimate.

In a further message, five days later, Sir Ian Hamilton stated that direct progress would be slow, and that he had been considering another line of operations starting from Enos, which he had rejected because of the objections of Sir John de Robeck.

Lord Kitchener's memorandum and the whole situation were considered by the Dardanelles Committee on June 7th, 1915, and the following conclusions were reached:

(1) To reinforce Sir Ian Hamilton with the three remaining divisions of the New Army, with a view to an assault in the second week of July.

(2) To send out certain naval units, which would be much less vulnerable to submarine attack than those under Admiral de Robeck's command.

There are no minutes of this meeting, but it is stated by Mr Churchill that the intention of the Committee was to authorise a more energetic prosecution of the operations than that mentioned in Lord Kitchener's third proposition of May 28th, and that Lord Kitchener himself said: "Do not let Sir Ian Hamilton throw away his strength in the interval, but let us send out ample reinforcements to carry the thing through." Lord Selborne agrees that the decision of the Dardanelles Committee contemplated a more vigorous continuation of the joint military and naval operations than the course proposed by Lord Kitchener.

Just after midnight on June 7th Sir Ian Hamilton sent a telegram reviewing the situation and emphasising the need for reinforcements.

> Without additional troops sufficient to provide for reliefs, as well as reinforcements, the men are undoubtedly getting worn out, and this will end in reducing our forces at Cape Helles to position of defenders in state of close siege, as is practically the case at Australian and New Zealand Army Corps already . . .
>
> In the action of June 4th the troops succeeded in breaking through the centre of the enemy's line, but were so weakened by the effort that they could not take advantage of success, nor even retain all the ground gained. The whole position might have been captured and a great step made in advance, had there been plenty of fresh reserves available to push through and confirm success.

Lord Kitchener had in fact a few hours earlier cabled to Sir Ian Hamilton assuring him that the Government intended to make due provision for reinforcements. The full text of the telegram is as follows:

> Your difficulties are fully recognised by the Cabinet, who are determined to support you. We are sending you three divisions of the New Army. The first of these will leave about the end of this week, and the other two will be sent as transport is available. The last of the three divisions ought to reach you not later than the first fortnight in July. While steadily

pressing the enemy, there seems no reason for
running any premature risks in the meantime.

As a matter of fact the embarkation of the 13th
Division took place from June 16th to June 23rd; of
the 11th Division from July 1st to July 7th; and of the
10th Division from July 7th to July 14th.

Another cause contributed at this time to weaken
the British troops and make the requests for reinforcements urgent. The weather had become very hot
and with the heat there came swarms of flies. On the
whole the sanitation of the British camps and
trenches was satisfactorily carried out so far as was
possible with the appliances which could be pro-
cured, but the Turkish trenches were very near, and
the state of them was very bad; there were many
unburied bodies, both of men and animals, at no great
distance, and it was found impossible to keep down
the plague of flies. These conveyed a great amount of
infection, and this was also disseminated by the dust
constantly carried about by the wind. The most common illness which resulted was a kind of dysentery,
though para-typhoid and other complaints prevailed.
Apart from reduction in numbers caused by death,
the force was seriously weakened by the number of
men always ill and the lowering of vitality produced
in those who were still on duty.

On June 9th the Cabinet confirmed the decision
of the Dardanelles Committee. This conclusion was
an acknowledgment that the attempt to seize the
peninsula by a rapid advance had failed; and that a

larger force, more continued operations, and greater supplies of ammunition would be necessary to obtain success.

Another meeting of the Dardanelles Committee was held on June 12th, 1915, at which the Prime Minister submitted for consideration a memorandum by Mr Ashmead Bartlett, who had been on the peninsula as a war correspondent. In this memorandum Mr Ashmead Bartlett expressed an unfavourable view of the positions then occupied at Anzac and Helles and of the prospects of success in an advance from those positions, and advised an attack at or near the isthmus of Bulair. The Committee decided to ask Sir Ian Hamilton for information on the matter, and a telegram was sent accordingly on June 12th. Sir Ian Hamilton answered on June 13th, giving his reasons against an attack in the neighbourhood of Bulair. He had sent substantially the same information the day before in answer to an enquiry from the War Office. These reasons seem to have satisfied the Committee, and an attack at Bulair was not further considered at that time.

It should be mentioned here that on June 21st Lord Kitchener had asked if Sir Ian Hamilton required a fourth division, and he had answered that he did not feel justified in refusing it, and that on June 25th Lord Kitchener had said that the Cabinet would like to know whether he considered it necessary or desirable that a fifth division should be sent. On June 29th Sir Ian Hamilton answered that, as the fourth and fifth divisions could not arrive with the first

three, he adhered to his original plan of trying to turn
the enemy's right at Anzac with the first three divisions and to gain a position from Kaba Tepe to
Maidos. He would use the fourth and fifth, in case of
non-success at first, to reinforce this wing; and in case
of success, possibly to push through from Helles, but
more probably to effect a landing on the southern
shore of the Dardanelles. He concluded:

> To summarise, I think I have reasonable prospects of
> success with three divisions, with four the risk of
> miscalculation would be minimised, and with five,
> even if the fifth division had little or no gun
> ammunition, I think it would be a much simpler
> matter to clear the Asiatic shore subsequently of big
> guns, i.e., Kilid Bahr would be captured at an earlier
> date, and success would be generally assured.

In accordance with the views expressed by Sir Ian
Hamilton, it was decided to send him a fifth as well as
a fourth division.

During July, Sir Ian Hamilton further considered
the scheme outlined in his telegram to Lord
Kitchener of June 29th and a definite plan of action
was elaborated under his orders.

This plan is described in Sir Ian Hamilton's
despatch of December 11th, 1915. In June he had
asked for and been promised a reinforcement consisting of three divisions of the New Army, to which the
infantry of two Territorial Divisions had been subsequently added. He expected all these troops to arrive

between July 10th and August 10th, and this anticipation was realised. After considering several other courses, he decided to employ a part of them to strengthen the Australian and New Zealand Army Corps at Anzac, and the remainder to effect a surprise landing in Suvla Bay. In his despatch Sir Ian Hamilton's objectives are defined as follows:

(1) To break out with a rush from Anzac and cut off the bulk of the Turkish Army from land communication with Constantinople.

(2) To gain such a command for my artillery as to cut off the bulk of the Turkish Army from sea traffic whether with Constantinople or with Asia.

(3) Incidentally, to secure Suvla Bay as a winter base for Anzac and all the troops operating in the northern theatre.

Sir Ian Hamilton determined that the operations should begin on August 6th, as the moon would then rise at an hour favourable for night landings, and the last of his reinforcements were due to arrive a day or two before that date. The plan is described in greater detail in the instructions issued by the Chief of the General Staff, Mediterranean Expeditionary Force, to the General Officer Commanding VIIIth Corps at Helles, and the General Officer Commanding IXth Corps at Imbros, dated July 29th, and to the General Officer Commanding Australian and New Zealand Army Corps at Anzac, dated July 30th.

At Helles the troops of the VIIIth Corps were to attack the Turks on August 4th and following days, not so much with a view to gaining ground in the direction of Krithia or Achi Baba as for the purpose of distracting the enemy's attention from the contemplated operations at Anzac and Suvla, and of preventing him from reinforcing the positions which it was intended to seize and occupy.

The operations at Anzac were held by Sir Ian Hamilton to be of primary importance, those at Helles and Suvla being described as complementary.

THE OPERATIONS IN MAY, JUNE AND JULY

In the meantime, fighting had continued on both the Anzac and Helles fronts. At Anzac severe fighting took place by reason of very heavy attacks made by the Turks. These attacks were defeated and some slight ground was gained, but it did not amount to more than straightening out short lengths of trench here and there and, broadly speaking, the force remained in the position which it had occupied on the day of landing.

At Helles, up to June 4th, only minor operations were undertaken, and small advances were made in parts of the lines, but on that day a great attack was made along the whole front from the Straits to the sea.

The attack was partially successful, and the Manchester Brigade and some companies of the 5th Lancashire Fusiliers and part of the 42nd Division, which arrived early in May, got nearly to Krithia, reaching a position favourable to an attack on Achi Baba.

Unfortunately, the Turks, by a counter-attack, were able to carry a redoubt called the Haricot, which had been taken from them at the first attack, and this redoubt enfiladed [sent a volley of gun-fire the length of] the positions won by the Naval Division on the right of the Manchester Brigade. It [the Naval Division] was obliged to fall back, uncovering the Manchester Brigade, which also had to retire. Sir Ian Hamilton speaks of the day as having promised great things, but ended disappointingly, and describes the result in the following terms:

> To sum up, a good advance of at least 500 yards, including two lines of Turkish trenches, has been made along a front of nearly three miles in the centre of our southern section, but we are back to our original right and left. Making fresh effort now to advance the left to bring it into line with the centre, though the Turkish position here is extraordinarily strong naturally, with a deep ravine on one side and the sea on the other.

On June 21st the French stormed the Haricot redoubt and repulsed the Turkish counter-attacks, and on June 28th another great attack was made by the British force, which had considerable success.

As described by Major-General de Lisle, commanding the 29th Division, an advance was made of about a mile, and five lines of trenches were taken. Sir Ian Hamilton speaks of this advance as running up level to Krithia. He says that, if he had had reinforcements and ammunition on the spot, the success could have been made decisive: "We had the Turks beaten then." But, naturally, the result of this continuous fighting had much exhausted and depleted the British troops, the stocks of ammunition were low, the drafts were coming forward very slowly, so that all units were much under strength, and no large reinforcements would arrive for some time. He was, therefore, unable to follow up the success, and during July only small operations took place. In the meantime the continuance of Russian reverses in Galicia encouraged the Turks, lessened their apprehension of a Russian landing near Constantinople, and enabled them to send up reinforcements.

On June 29th and 30th a heavy attack was made on the Anzac position and was repulsed.

Details of these operations will be found in Sir Ian Hamilton's despatch of August 26th, 1915, published in the *London Gazette Supplement* of September 20th, 1915.

On June 22nd Lord Kitchener sent the following description of the Divisions of the New Army to Sir Ian Hamilton:

> The three divisions being sent to you are well trained with fine personnel. From the training point of view, there is not much to choose between them, but they might be placed in the following order—11th, 13th, 10th. The infantry is excellent, and their shooting good. The artillery have fired well. The RE, RAMC, and ASC are above the average. You will understand that the new officers' knowledge is not yet instinctive, and allowance should be made for this by the staff; if so, in a short time there will be no finer troops in Europe. Upon the personality of the commander, of course, will depend the choice of divisions for any particular operation.

It will be seen that for new troops a high character was given to them, and possibly this was the main reason why the landing at Suvla was entrusted to a portion of them without the help of more experienced troops. A night attack in an unknown country was a difficult task for inexperienced soldiers, and they would have been much strengthened by an admixture of more seasoned units. The fourth and fifth divisions (the 53rd Welsh and 54th East Anglian) consisted of Territorial troops.

SELECTION OF OFFICERS

At this point it will be convenient to refer to the selection of a commander for the IXth Corps, which consisted of the 10th, 11th and 13th Divisions, and of commanders for those divisions and the two Territorial divisions.

On June 15th Sir Ian Hamilton had submitted to Lord Kitchener his opinion of the qualities necessary for a Corps Commander on the Gallipoli Peninsula in these words: "In that position only men of good, stiff constitution and nerve will be able to do any good." To secure such qualities it would have been advantageous to select some officer who had proved the possession of them in the fighting of the previous ten months. Most of these officers, however, were employed on the Western Front, and could not easily be replaced. The difficulty was increased by the fact that Sir Bryan Mahon, who commanded the 10th Division, was a Lieutenant-General.

Sir Ian Hamilton asked for one of two Lieutenant-Generals then in France, Sir Julian Byng or Sir Henry Rawlinson, but neither could be spared. The former was sent to take over the command of the IXth Corps after the failure at Suvla. There may have been reasons for allowing him to leave France then which did not exist in June, but had it been possible it might, perhaps, have been better to appoint him in the first instance. In the result the choice practically lay between Sir Frederick Stopford and another Lieutenant-General whom Sir Ian Hamilton considered for physical reasons to be unsuited for trench warfare, and Sir Frederick Stopford was appointed. It is only to this extent that Sir Ian Hamilton can be said to have asked for Sir Frederick Stopford.

Sir Frederick Stopford was an officer with a good record, but he had not been actively employed for some time.

The qualifications mentioned by Sir Ian Hamilton would apply equally to the Divisional Commanders. As regards these we find little or nothing in the evidence that reflects on the capacity for command in the field of Sir Bryan Mahon, who had trained and commanded the 10th Division in Ireland. Major-General Hammersley had similarly trained and commanded the 11th Division, upon which the heaviest of the fighting at Suvla fell, and in ordinary course he took out his division to the Gallipoli Peninsula. We think this was unfortunate, as he had suffered from a breakdown some two years before; and although he had apparently recovered, his previous illness may account for the want of promptitude and decision which, we regret to say, he appears to have shown when faced by what were, no doubt, exceptional difficulties.

The 13th Division was commanded by Major-General F. C. Shaw, who proved himself to be well qualified for the appointment. Sir Ian Hamilton detached this division from the IXth Corps and placed it at Sir William Birdwood's disposal. Major-General the Hon. J. E. Lindley commanded the 53rd

Territorial Division. The division was much split up and disintegrated as soon as it landed at Suvla, and on August 17th he resigned the command, his reason being that he understood Sir Ian Hamilton to be dissatisfied with him and thought that his division might have a better chance under another commander. Major-General F. S. Inglefield, commanding the 54th Territorial Division, was 60 years old when he took out the division to the Gallipoli Peninsula, and at this age was, perhaps, hardly equal to the strain of field service under specially arduous conditions.

THE OPERATIONS IN AUGUST AT HELLES AND ANZAC

The operations in August were, as we have already said, divided into three attacks: one at Helles, one at Anzac, and one at Suvla. These attacks were made by three distinct forces not in direct communication with one another. The control of operations so divided was difficult, and Sir Ian Hamilton decided that the best position from which he could exercise such control was Imbros, where he had his headquarters. He was then in cable communication with the three Corps Headquarters, and could reach any one of them in less than an hour. This choice of Imbros has been criticised, but we think that the reasons given for it are satisfactory.

HELLES

The attack at Helles was made on the same day as the other attacks—August 6th, 1915. Its scope and form were, as has been said, to be determined solely with reference to its effects on the main operations, and it was directed against certain Turkish trenches mentioned in the Instructions to General Officer Commanding, VIIIth Corps. Unfortunately, when it was made these trenches were found to be occupied by a very strong force of Turks collected there for the purpose of an attack on the British position. The British attack on that day failed, but fighting continued for about a week, the severest taking place round what was called the Vineyard, a plot of ground 200 yards long by 100 yards wide. No substantial success was obtained by this fighting so far as an advance was concerned, but the result was to keep the Turkish troops in that part engaged and to draw some reinforcements from other parts of the peninsula which could otherwise have been employed at Anzac or Suvla. In view of the fact that the Turks were in sufficient force to resist the attacks at Anzac and Suvla, we think the value to be attached to the subsidiary operations at Helles must remain problematical.

ANZAC

The operations at Anzac and Suvla were more closely connected with one another than with those at Helles. Certain times were specified at which important points were to be occupied. We are of the opinion that, considering the nature of the country, it was impossible to rely upon this time-table being carried out, but we do not think that the accurate carrying out of the time-table was vital to the general success of the operations. The principal assistance to be given to the Anzac Force by the troops landing at Suvla was the seizure of Yilghin Burnu and Ismail Oglu Tepe, on account of the presence there of artillery likely to interfere with the Anzac Force, and any other help by moving troops up the slopes of Sari Bahr was only to be given, if possible, after the fulfilment of the primary mission of the General Officer Commanding IXth Corps, i.e., securing Suvla Bay as a base. In fact, Ismail Oglu Tepe was never occupied, but we have not any evidence to show that the presence of artillery on that hill had any material effect on the Anzac attack.

For the purpose of the attack from Anzac, General Birdwood's force had been reinforced by the 13th Division, the 29th Brigade of the 10th Division, and the 29th (Indian) Brigade. These had been taken over to the peninsula at night and concealed in dug-outs near the shore so that they might escape the notice of the Turks. This operation seems to have been carried out with credit to those engaged in it, and to the Dominion troops who prepared the dug-outs.

Sir William Birdwood had under his command 37,000 rifles and 72 guns, and he could count on naval support from two cruisers, four monitors, and two destroyers. The force was divided into two main portions—one (consisting of the Australian Division together with the 1st and 3rd Light Horse Brigades and two battalions of the 40th Brigade) which was to hold the existing position and make frontal attacks from it; the other (consisting of the New Zealand and Australian Division, less the 1st and 3rd Light Horse Brigades, the 13th Division less five battalions, the 29th Indian Infantry Brigade, and the Indian Mountain Artillery Brigade) which was to attack the Chunuk Bahr ridge. The 29th Brigade of the 10th Division less one battalion and the 38th Brigade were in reserve.

About 5 pm on August 6th, the operations began by an attack on the position known as Lone Pine, its main object being to divert the enemy's attention and reserves from the principal attack on the Sari Bahr heights. The position is described by Sir Ian Hamilton as having been strongly entrenched and obstinately held. According to his despatch it was carried with great gallantry by the Australian troops, and held against counter-attacks which were continued until August 12th. The assault on Lone Pine was presumably effective in keeping a considerable Turkish force from opposing the main attack on the Sari Bahr heights.

It may be mentioned here that two minor attacks were also made with the same object as the attack on Lone Pine, namely, to distract the enemy's attention from the main attack on the Sari Bahr heights. The first of these minor attacks took place at midnight on the 6th, and was directed on a Turkish trench opposite the extreme right of the Anzac front; the second took place at 4.30 am on the 7th, and was directed on a point called Baby 700, just north of Hill 180, opposite the centre of the Anzac front. Both these attacks were repulsed with heavy loss.

Beginning at 9.30 pm on the 6th, the flanking or encircling movement on the Chunuk Bahr ridge and Sari Bahr was made in two covering and two attacking columns. The constitution of these columns and the tasks assigned to them are thus described in the despatch:

> It was our object to effect a lodgment* along the crest of the high main ridge with two columns of troops, but, seeing the nature of the ground and the dispositions of the enemy, the effort had to be made by stages. We were bound, in fact, to undertake a double subsidiary operation before we could hope to launch these attacks with any real prospect of success.
>
> (1) The right covering force was to seize Table Top, as well as all other enemy positions commanding the foothills between the Chailak Dere and the Sazli Beit Dere ravines. If this enterprise succeeded it would

---

* A position defended against the besieging party.

open up the ravines for the assaulting columns, whilst at the same time interposing between the right flank of the left covering force and the enemy holding the Sari Bahr main ridge.

(2) The left covering force was to march northwards along the beach to seize a hill called Damakjelik Bahr, some 1,400 yards north of Table Top. If success-ful it would be able to hold out a hand to the IXth Corps as it landed south of Nebrunesi Point, whilst at the same time protecting the left flank of the left assaulting column against enemy troops from the Anafarta valley during its climb up the Aghyl Dere ravine.

(3) The right assaulting column was to move up the Chailak Dere and Sazli Beit Dere ravines to the storm of the ridge of Chunuk Bahr.

(4) The left assaulting column was to work up the Aghyl Dere and prolong the line of the right assaulting col-umn by storming Hill 305 (Koja Chemen Tepe), the summit of the whole range of hills.

To recapitulate, the two assaulting columns, which were to work up three ravines to the storm of the high ridge, were to be preceded by two covering columns. One of these was to capture the enemy's positions commanding the foothills, first to open the mouths of the ravines, secondly to cover the right flank of another covering force whilst it marched along the beach. The other covering column was to strike far out to the north until, from a hill called Damakjelik Bahr, it could at the same time facilitate the landing of the IXth Corps at Nebrunesi Point, and guard the left flank of the column assaulting Sari Bahr from any forces of the enemy which might be assembled in the Anafarta valley.

The whole of this big attack was placed under the command of Major-General Sir Alexander J. Godley, General Officer Commanding New Zealand and Australian Division. The two covering and the two assaulting columns were organized as follows:

Right Covering Column, under Brigadier-General A. H. Russell—New Zealand Mounted Rifles Brigade, the Otago Mounted Rifles Regiment, the Maori Contingent and New Zealand Field Troop.

Right Assaulting Column, under Brigadier-General F. E. Johnston—New Zealand Infantry Brigade, Indian Mountain Battery (less one section), one Company New Zealand Engineers.

Left Covering Column, under Brigadier-General J. H. Travers—Headquarters 40th Brigade, half the 72nd Field Company, 4th Battalion South Wales Borderers, and 5th Battalion Wiltshire Regiment.

Left Assaulting Column, under Brigadier-General (now Major-General) H.V. Cox—29th Indian Infantry Brigade, 4th Australian Infantry Brigade, Indian Mountain Battery (less one section), one Company New Zealand Engineers.

Divisional Reserve—6th Battalion South Lancashire Regiment and 8th Battalion Welsh Regiment (Pioneers) at Chailak Dere, and the 39th Infantry Brigade and half 72nd Field Company at Aghyl Dere.

The right covering column took Old No. 3 Post and Table Top, both of them stated to be positions of great strength, and so opened up the Sazli Beit Dere and also cleared the Chailak Dere; in doing so it had to pass a barbed wire obstacle of a formidable nature. It also occupied Bauchop's Hill, described as a "maze of ridge and ravine everywhere entrenched."

The left covering column advanced up the Aghyl Dere, rushing the Turkish trenches on the way, and occupied Damakjelik Bahr, thus protecting the left rear of the whole Anzac attack.

The right assaulting column advancing over difficult country reached Rhododendron Spur, a point 500 yards west of Chunuk Bahr.

The left assaulting column advanced up the Aghyl Dere, which divides into a northern and southern branch, and one half of the column followed the northern half and got across into the northern end of the Azma Dere ravine. The other half followed the southern branch and reached the lower slopes of Hill Q, a point on the Sari Bahr ridge a little lower than the highest point—Koja Chemen Tepe—and separated from it by a deep ravine.

This was the position on the afternoon of August 7th, and that evening the force was re-organized for a fresh advance to take place on the early morning of the 8th. The despatch states:

The columns were composed as follows:
Right Column, Brigadier-General F. E. Johnston—
26th Indian Mountain Battery (less one section),

Auckland Mounted Rifles, New Zealand Infantry
Brigade, two Battalions 13th Division, and the Maori
Contingent.

Centre and Left Columns—Major-General H.V.
Cox—21st Indian Mountain Battery (less one
section), 4th Australian Brigade, 39th Infantry
Brigade (less one battalion), with 6th Battalion South
Lancashire Regiment attached, and the 29th Indian
Infantry Brigade.

The right column was to climb up the Chunuk
Bahr ridge; the left column was to make for the
prolongation of the ridge north-east to Koja Chemen
Tepe, the topmost peak of the range.

On August 8th the only important success was
attained by the right column, which succeeded in
occupying Chunuk Bahr, an important position,
though it was not one from which the Straits could
be seen. The centre and left columns met with such
heavy opposition that they were unable to make any
material advance, and the left suffered so heavily that
it had to be withdrawn to its original position.

On August 9th, 1915, the attack was renewed,
with the troops again re-arranged in three columns,
whose constitution and objectives were thus
described:

The columns for the renewed attack were composed
as follows:

No. 1 Column, Brigadier-General F. E. Johnston—
26th Indian Mountain Battery (less one section), the

Auckland and Wellington Mounted Rifles
Regiments, the New Zealand Infantry Brigade, and
two battalions of the 13th Division.

No. 2 Column, Major-General H.V. Cox—21st
Indian Mountain Battery (less one section), 4th
Australian Brigade, 39th Brigade (less the 7th
Gloucesters, relieved), with the 6th Battalion South
Lancashire Regiment attached, and the Indian
Infantry Brigade.

No. 3 Column, Brigadier-General A. H. Baldwin,
commanding 38th Infantry Brigade—two battalions
each from the 38th and 29th Brigades and one from
the 40th Brigade.

No. 1 Column was to hold and consolidate the
ground gained on the 6th, and, in co-operation with
the other columns, to gain the whole of Chunuk
Bahr, and extend to the south-east. No. 2 Column was
to attack Hill Q on the Chunuk Bahr ridge, and No. 3
Column was to move from the Chailak Dere, also on
Hill Q. This last column was to make the main attack,
and the others were to co-operate with it.

A part of No. 1 Column, under the command of
Major, now Lieutenant-Colonel Allanson, consisting
of a detachment of the 6th Gurkhas and of the 6th
South Lancashire Regiment (450 strong), succeeded
in getting to a point on the ridge from which the
Straits and the country on the far side could be seen.
The exact point which they reached is not quite
clearly ascertained, but it probably was at or near the
top of the Chunuk Bahr ridge, near the highest point,

which is called Koja Chemen Tepe. From this point the Narrows could be seen.

They were afterwards driven back by artillery fire to the trenches in which they had been the night before, and later in the day were counter-attacked by the Turks in force and driven down the hill.

The suggestion has been made that this artillery fire came from the British ships, and Lieutenant-Colonel Allanson inclined to this view. But Colonel Allanson's account is that the salvo [artillery attack] struck his men when they were pursuing the Turks a short distance down the reverse slope; and we accept Sir William Birdwood's opinion that, if the Gurkhas were on the reverse slope near the crest, it would have been impossible for naval guns to hit them. We do not think it possible to say whether the shells were Turkish or came from the high-angle fire of our howitzers putting a barrage on the reverse slopes. As Sir Alexander Godley remarks, it is often not possible in a modern battle to be quite certain as to particular facts.

No. 3 column, under Brigadier-General Baldwin, which was attacking the same ridge from another direction, was unfortunately deflected to the left, in the direction of a place called The Farm, and never reached the ridge. In Sir Ian Hamilton's despatch it is said that Brigadier-General Baldwin, through no fault of his own, owing to the darkness and the awful country, lost his way. Sir Alexander Godley thinks it possible that General Baldwin did not exactly lose his way, but was driven rather to the left on to the lower slopes leading to The Farm by the heavy rifle and machine-gun fire which was sweeping the higher ground up which he should have gone. General Baldwin, with most of his staff, was killed very soon afterwards, and therefore it is impossible to ascertain what actually occurred.

No progress of any importance had been made from Suvla, and there was nothing in the operations in that area to divert the Turkish reinforcements from Sari Bahr. Thus the counter-attacks in that direction, which finally drove the British troops from the ridge, could be made in full strength.

General Baldwin, on arriving at The Farm, and finding that he could not reach the ridge according to the original plan, deployed his attack where he was, and some of his men charged up their side of the slope. The Turks, who were in overwhelming numbers, drove them back to The Farm, and then attacked the New Zealand troops which were holding Chunuk Bahr; but the New Zealanders, though much exhausted, continued to hold the position until relieved during the night.

On August 10th, 1915, the Turks, in great strength, attacked Chunuk Bahr and carried it. They also turned the flank of General Baldwin's column, and drove it from its position. It was in this fighting that General Baldwin and all his staff were killed. Reserves were sent up and the Turks driven back, but they kept their hold on Chunuk Bahr.

Sir Ian Hamilton says that he thought at one time of throwing his reserves into the Anzac battle, but was prevented from doing so because he feared that the water supply at Anzac would not be sufficient for a larger number of troops. Sir William Birdwood told us that he did not think he could have provided water for more troops; but it seems doubtful, in any case, if the reserves could have been put into the fighting line in time to save the situation.

REASONS FOR FAILURE

The country over which these operations were carried out was extremely difficult. General Cox describes it in this way:

> It was an extraordinarily difficult bit of country and a confused country. There does not seem to be any reason why the hills should go where they do. It has been done by tremendous rushes of water. It is mad-looking country and very difficult.

The ground was very steep and without paths or tracks, broken up into gullies and tangled hollows, and covered with thick scrub. The weather, too, was very hot, and the climate very trying, even to the Australian and New Zealand troops, who had been acclimatised for several months; and much more so to the British troops, who had not been long out of England. A very hard task was therefore set to the troops. Sir William Birdwood, who presumably knew the country so far as it could be known, thought that the attack ought to succeed, and that the difficulties of the country would help him to surprise the Turks; and both he and Lieutenant-General Godley ascribe the failure to the Turks being in too strong force. Sir William Birdwood says: "They were too strong for us. They were just too strong, but only just, because we got up there in two places, but we could not maintain ourselves." Sir Alexander Godley says "The enemy was too strong for us."

THE OPERATIONS AT SUVLA

We think it is necessary to review in some detail the operations at Suvla, as these have given rise to controversy between the principal officers concerned, and led to the removal from their commands of the Commander of the IXth Corps, one of the Divisional Commanders, and one of the Brigade Commanders.

OBJECTIVES

The outline of Sir Ian Hamilton's plans for a landing at Suvla and subsequent operations is contained in a letter dated July 22nd, 1915, from the Chief of the General Staff of the Mediterranean Force to the General Officer Commanding the IXth Corps. In this letter the strength of the enemy north of Kilid Bahr was estimated at 30,000; 12,000 occupying trenches opposite the Anzac position and most of the remainder being in reserve at Boghali, Kojadere, and Eski-Keui. There were believed to be three battalions in the Anafarta villages, one battalion at Ismail Oglu Tepe, one battalion on Chocolate Hill, and outposts at Lala Baba and Ghazi Baba. The ridge of Karakol Dagh and Kiretch Tepe Sirt was understood to be held by gendarmerie. It was further stated that at or near Chocolate Hill and Ismail Oglu Tepe there were one 9.2 inch gun, one 4.7 inch gun, and three field guns, protected by wire entanglements and infantry trenches. Three field guns were reported later as having been seen moving into Anafarta Sagir.

On July 29th further instructions, which appear among the appendices to Sir Ian Hamilton's despatch, were issued to the General Officer Commanding the IXth Corps. Therein it was laid down that the primary objective would be to secure Suvla Bay as a base for all forces operating in the northern zone, and that, owing to the difficult nature of the terrain at Suvla, the attainment of this objective might possibly require the use of all the troops at Sir Frederick Stopford's disposal. If, however, troops could be spared, his next step should be to assist the General Officer Commanding at Anzac in the latter's attack on Koja Chemen Tepe by an advance on Buyuk Anafarta. Subject only to his final approval, Sir Ian Hamilton gave Sir Frederick Stopford a free hand in regard to the plan of military operations at Suvla, and the latter was requested to submit a plan for approval as soon as possible.

The plan was submitted in a letter dated July 31st, 1915, and met with Sir Ian Hamilton's full approval. In this letter Sir Frederick Stopford recorded his conviction that to secure the reasonable immunity of Suvla Bay from shell fire, the occupation of the high ground from Ejelmer Bay to Anafarta Sagir and thence to Koja Chemen Tepe was essential. He also laid stress on the improbability of his being able to spare troops to assist the Anzac force in the attack on Koja Chemen Tepe.

THE OPERATION ORDER

On receipt of Sir Ian Hamilton's approval, Sir Frederick Stopford issued an Operation Order, dated August 3rd, 1915, in which the following task was assigned to General Hammersley:

(*a*) To safeguard the landing places.
(*b*) To occupy the enemy posts of Lala Baba and Ghazi Baba, and to establish a footing along the ridge from Ghazi Baba through Karakol Dagh

and Kiretch Tepe Sirt to Hill 156, immediately overlooking Ejelmer Bay.

(*c*) To occupy Chocolate Hill and Ismail Oglu Tepe.

(*d*) To seize Baka Baba and establish connection northwards between that point and the troops advancing on Hill 156.

This was an extremely ambitious programme for one division, and only part of it was carried into effect. It is noticeable in this operation order that, although the two brigades of the 10th Division were mentioned in the list of available troops, no reference was made to the divisional commander, Sir Bryan Mahon, a Lieutenant-General of considerable seniority, nor was any duty assigned to these brigades.

General Braithwaite's letter and instructions of July 22nd and 29th, and Sir Frederick Stopford's Operation Order of August 3rd, give the following information in regard to the units detailed for the Suvla operations. According to the letter of July 22nd the force placed at Sir Frederick Stopford's disposal for the landing was to consist of the 11th Division under General Hammersley, the 10th Division (less the 29th Brigade) under Sir Bryan Mahon, two batteries of Highland Mountain Artillery, and the 1/4th Lowland Howitzer Brigade. The table appended to the letter includes, among the divisional troops of the 11th Division, two out of three Brigades of Field Artillery and one Heavy Battery, the third Brigade of Field Artillery having been landed at Helles. No mention is made in the table of the Divisional Artillery of the 10th Division.

In the instructions of July 29th the Lowland Howitzer Brigade was omitted, and three squadrons of the RN Armoured Car Division, RNAS, each armed with six machine guns, were added. It was stated that the following units were being despatched from Alexandria: the three squadrons of the RN Armoured Car Division, three Brigades of Field Artillery belonging to the 10th Division, one Brigade of Field Artillery belonging to the 11th Division, and two Brigades of Field Artillery belonging to the 13th Division. As one Brigade of Field Artillery belonging to the 11th Division had been landed at Helles, it would appear that only one Brigade of Field Artillery was actually attached at the time to that division.

In the Operation Order of August 3rd it was stated that one Brigade of Field Artillery belonging to the 11th Division and one Heavy Battery with their horses would land at Anzac, and proceed thence along the beach to join the division on its landing at Suvla. The two Highland Mountain Batteries and one squadron of the RN Armoured Car Division (motor cycles) were to land at Suvla. There is no record of the date and place of landing of the other two squadrons of the RN Armoured Car Division, which consisted of Ford cars and armoured cars.

AVAILABLE ARTILLERY

The question of the artillery actually available at Suvla is discussed in a "Statement in connection with Sir Ian Hamilton's despatch of 11th December, 1915." This statement was drawn up by Sir Frederick Stopford by direction of the Adjutant-General, and is dated February 16th, 1916. The relevant paragraph is as follows:

> As regards other points in Sir Ian Hamilton's despatch which affect the IXth Corps, the description of the troops at my disposal is incorrectly stated. He states that at my disposal 'was placed the IXth Army Corps, less the 13th Division and the 29th Brigade of the 10th Division.' He should have stated that the 10th Division had no artillery, and that of the artillery of the 11th Division only one brigade of artillery was available until 12th August, and of it only one battery was available for the fighting of August 7th–8th.

Further information on the subject is given in General Braithwaite's instructions which were handed to General de Lisle on August 15th, when the latter called at Imbros on his way to replace Sir Frederick Stopford in the command of the IXth Corps. It would appear that at that date the artillery actually available at Suvla consisted of two mountain and two heavy batteries, and one brigade of field artillery.

Sir Frederick Stopford's contention as to the paucity of artillery is in substance supported by the evidence of General de Lisle.

TOPOGRAPHY

And here it may be convenient to attempt some description of the ground in the vicinity of Suvla Bay. The area bordering the Salt Lake is low, and doubtless swampy in wet weather. In the dry season it is bare and open until the ground begins to rise. Then high grass and bush appear, the bush being mostly a prickly variety of *Ilex* [holly], very hard and tough. The bush in many cases increases in density and height as the hills get higher. The country can hardly be described as well watered during the dry season, but a moderate amount of water is procurable by those who know where to look for it and how to get it.

The following remarks by Sir Ian Hamilton on the nature of the ground at and near Suvla are of interest. In a letter to Lord Kitchener, dated August 12th, 1915, he wrote:

> The whole of the flattish plain east of Suvla Bay is covered with thick trees up high above your head, small and big dongas [gullies], long grass, etc. In these a very considerable number of Turkish snipers are concealed, sometimes up in the trees, sometimes down in hollows among the grass ... Supposing the Essex [161st Brigade of the 54th Division] make good their footing on the high hills north of Anafarta, there will

always remain the problem of getting their mule convoys through this dense bush without being too much harried or losing too many mules.

Again, in a letter to Lord Kitchener, dated September 1st, 1915, he described the Suvla Bay country as "a jungle ringed round by high mountains." Again in his despatch of December 11th, 1915, he referred to Ismail Oglu Tepe as follows:

> The hill rises 350 feet from the plain with steep spurs jutting out to the west and south-west, the whole of it covered with dense holly oak scrub, so nearly impenetrable that it breaks up an attack and forces troops to move in single file along goat tracks between the bushes.

In the same despatch, describing an attack on August 12th by the 163rd Brigade on Kuchuk Anafarta Ova, about 2,000 yards north-east of the north-east corner of the Salt Lake, he records the mysterious disappearance of the commanding officer, 16 officers, and 250 men of the 1/5th Norfolk Regiment, who charged into the forest, were lost to sight or sound, and never reappeared.

In his evidence before us Sir Ian Hamilton gave the following description:

> The actual heights to get up were difficult. They were hills very thickly clothed with scrub and jungle with paths, but rather difficult for a man with his

pack on to force his way through; but all the background of the bay was too open and too flat. It had one great advantage, that it was the only part of the peninsula where the guns of the ships could really command the ground.

Taking into consideration this and other evidence bearing on the subject, it may, we think, be concluded that the country in the vicinity of Suvla Bay must seriously have impeded military operations, more particularly in the way of breaking up concerted movements, and rendering night operations hazardous if not almost impracticable. The ground east of Anzac was more intricate and more broken, but the natural difficulties at Suvla were of a formidable character.

LANDING OPERATIONS ON AUGUST 6TH/7TH

The impression conveyed by the Intelligence reports which were communicated to Sir Frederick Stopford and Major-General Hammersley was that little opposition would be met with on landing except perhaps at Lala Baba, until the occupation of Chocolate Hill and Ismail Oglu Tepe was attempted. The time of landing was fixed for the evening of August 6th, and in drafting his divisional orders Major General Hammersley had to consider whether Chocolate Hill and Ismail Oglu Tepe should be attacked from the north-west or south-west. He decided in favour of the former alternative. His orders to the three brigades of his division were as follows:

> The 34th Brigade on the left to land at the original Beach A 800 yards west of Hill 10; one battalion to move north towards Kiretch Tepe Sirt and occupy Suvla Point; one battalion to occupy Hill 10; the remaining two battalions to concentrate at Hill 10. These three battalions at Hill 10 then to move to the assault of Chocolate Hill, and if successful, to the assault of Ismail Oglu Tepe.
>
> The 32nd Brigade in the centre to land at Beach C; to assault and occupy Lala Baba, and then move north along the sand-spit in support of the 34th Brigade.
>
> The 33rd Brigade on the right to land at Beach B about a mile south-east of Nebrunesi Point; two battalions to hold the line from the south-east corner of the Salt Lake south-westerly to the shore. Two battalions to follow the 32nd Brigade along the sand-spit to a point 800 yards east of Hill 10, there to form the divisional reserve with the divisional Pioneer Battalion (6th East Yorkshire Regiment).
>
> The artillery to concentrate at Lala Baba, where the divisional report centre was to be established.

For the transport of the division from Imbros ten destroyers and ten lighters★ were allotted—three of each for each brigade, and one of each for divisional

---

★ Large, open boats used for loading/unloading ships.

headquarters, signal section, cyclists, and engineers. From 500 to 550 men were embarked on each destroyer and lighter, and there was much congestion, especially on the lighters. The men went on board on the afternoon of the 6th, and were on board with no room to move about from six to eight hours before disembarking. Some reserve ammunition and water were carried on the lighters, but, for reasons mentioned in that portion of our report which deals with the water arrangements, the water was not distributed, and on the disembarkation of the men the lighters at once left the shore.

The flotilla was ready and started at 6.30 pm. The Pioneer Battalion, one battery of Royal Field Artillery, and the 4th Highland Mountain Brigade of two batteries followed later. At 10.30 pm the flotilla arrived opposite the points of disembarkation. The disembarkation of the 34th Brigade did not work smoothly. The original Beach A proved unsuitable for landing owing to reefs, and the brigade actually landed towards the south end of the sand spit instead of opposite Hill 10, the lighters grounding some 100 yards from shore. The landing was opposed by shrapnel fire from Hill 10 and rifle fire from Lala Baba and the sand spit. The 11th Manchester Regiment moved along the beach towards Suvla Point and Karakol Dagh, and carried out the task assigned to it.

Brigadier-General Sitwell, commanding the 34th Brigade, landed about 3.30 am on the 7th and directed the 9th Lancashire Fusiliers to assault Hill 10. The battalion proceeded after some delay and confusion in that direction, and occupied the highest sand dune north of the Cut, under the impression that this dune was Hill 10. The remaining two battalions of the 34th Brigade began to land on the sand spit about 2.30 am on the 7th and their landing was completed by 5 am.

At 11 pm on the 6th August the two leading battalions of the 32nd Brigade landed at a point between B and C beaches, and after considerable resistance Lala Baba was occupied. The remaining two battalions followed and concentrated at Lala Baba. This brigade was commanded by Brigadier-General Haggard.

Immediately after landing on the 7th Brigadier-General Sitwell asked for assistance from Brigadier-General Haggard, who sent a detachment from Lala Baba along the sand spit towards the Cut.

The 33rd Brigade, under Brigadier-General Maxwell, landed at Beach B without opposition. Two battalions took up and entrenched a line from the south-east corner of the Salt Lake south-westerly to the shore. The remaining two battalions proceeded to Lala Baba with a view to occupying subsequently their assigned position east of Hill 10 as a divisional reserve.

Shortly before daylight much desultory fighting took place between the Cut and Hill 10. Several isolated attempts to capture Hill 10 failed and the troops engaged fell back towards the Cut. Meanwhile, General Haggard had joined General Sitwell, the latter being the senior Brigade Commander in the division. By 6 am a fresh attack on Hill 10 was organised, the force being drawn from the 32nd and 34th Brigades. This attack succeeded, the Turks retiring in a north-easterly direction.

At 6.30 am General Sitwell reported to the Divisional Commander that his troops could not move eastward, this message apparently not reaching General Hammersley before 8 am.

We must now turn to the landing of the 10th Division, less one brigade detached to Anzac; this division being commanded by Lt.-General Sir Bryan Mahon.

It was originally intended that the two available brigades, the 30th and 31st, commanded respectively by Brigadier-Generals Nicol and Hill, together with the divisional Pioneer Battalion, should land at Beach A due west of Hill 10. This beach proved impracticable for landing, and a suitable place called New Beach A was eventually found in a cove about a mile east of Suvla Point and about 1,000 yards east of Ghazi Baba. On the arrival of the 10th Division from England between July 16th and 21st six battalions, namely, two battalions of the 30th Brigade and the whole of the 31st Brigade, had been sent to Mitylene under General Hill, the remaining two battalions of the 30th Brigade under General Nicol, plus the divisional Pioneer Battalion, being at Mudros, where the divisional Commander with his headquarters also was.

Sir Bryan Mahon received instructions about the Suvla landing on July 28th or 29th, but having failed to obtain a vessel to convey him to Mitylene he was unable to give any personal orders regarding disembarkation and subsequent action to General Hill, and his endeavour to communicate orders by cypher telegram failed. None of the artillery of the 10th Division landed until August 10th.

General Hill, followed by his six battalions, arrived at Suvla from Mitylene at daylight on August 7th, and was at once summoned to the *Jonquil*, where he saw Sir Frederick Stopford at about 6 am. He was directed by the latter to land at Beach C, to get in touch with the General Officer commanding the 11th Division, and to act under his orders. If he failed to get in touch, he was to advance and support the troops of the 11th Division and also to make good the occupation of Ghazi Baba and Karakol Dagh. Having selected a place west of Lala Baba for his troops to form up, General Hill went to the headquarters of the 11th Division and saw General Hammersley at about 8 am, who directed him, as soon as his troops were landed and concentrated, to move out along the sand-spit to the north-west corner of the Salt Lake, and thence to make an attack on Chocolate Hill, his right resting on the Salt Lake and his left being covered by troops of the 32nd and 34th Brigades, which would operate towards Ismail Oglu Tepe.

It must be mentioned here that only five out of the six battalions from Mitylene actually landed on August 7th at Beach C. One of the battalions of the 31st Brigade arrived too late on the 7th to join the force under General Hill and was sent across the bay to New Beach A, where it landed on the afternoon of the 7th or the morning of the 8th and came for the time being under the orders of General Nicol commanding the 30th Brigade. Sir Bryan Mahon with the headquarters of the 10th Division, General Nicol with his brigade staff, two battalions of the 30th Brigade, and the divisional Pioneer Battalion landed early on the morning of August 7th at New Beach A. Previous to landing Sir Bryan Mahon saw Sir Frederick Stopford, who ordered him to push on as far as possible along the ridge of Karakol Dagh and Kiretch Tepe Sirt in the direction of Ejelmer Bay. These orders were carried out so far as the small force at Sir Bryan Mahon's disposal would permit. The 11th Manchester Regiment, which was a battalion of the 34th Brigade, and which after occupying Suvla Point had advanced up Karakol Dagh before Sir Bryan Mahon's landing, took part in the movement along the ridge.

OPERATIONS ON AUGUST 7TH

From the foregoing account it will be seen that on the morning of August 7th the force at Suvla was allocated as follows by the Corps Commander: at the disposal of Major-General Hammersley, the whole of the 11th Division, less one battalion of the 34th Brigade (11th Manchester Regiment), plus five battalions of the 10th Division under Brigadier-General Hill; at the disposal of Lieutenant-General Sir Bryan Mahon two battalions of one of his brigades (the 30th Brigade) plus his divisional Pioneer Battalion, plus one battalion of the

34th Brigade of the 11th Division (the 11th Manchester Regiment). It will also be observed that the change in the scheme for distributing the troops when landed at Suvla on August 6th and 7th was largely due to the impracticability of disembarkation at the original Beach A and the unavoidable delay which occurred in finding the new Beach A.

It will further be noticed that the advance up Karakol Dagh and Kiretch Tepe Sirt, which had been assigned by the Corps Commander to Major-General Hammersley, was in fact undertaken by Sir Bryan Mahon.

At 8.45 am General Sitwell, whose report centre was south of Hill 10, received orders from General Hammersley for the 32nd and 34th Brigades to push on towards Chocolate Hill on the arrival of the 31st Brigade, which would operate on the left, moving with its own right on Ismail Oglu Tepe. This message apparently emanated from the divisional report centre at Lala Baba, at 8 am, at which hour General Hammersley had seen General Hill and told him to operate on the right of the 32nd and 34th Brigades with Chocolate Hill as his objective. At 8.55 am General Sitwell communicated the order he had just received to the commanders of three battalions of his own brigade, but gave no instructions to the 32nd Brigade, possibly because General Hammersley's orders had been repeated to General Haggard, the commander of that brigade.

Shortly afterwards General Sitwell, on his own initiative, directed two battalions of the 32nd

Brigade to form an entrenchment from Hill 10 to the Cut. Their employment in this manner seems to us to have been inconsistent with General Hammersley's order, and to have shown on General Sitwell's part a lack of the offensive spirit necessary to success.

Meanwhile at about 10 am three battalions out of the five under General Hill's command had landed and concentrated near Lala Baba. Having given instructions to the commanding officers of these battalions, General Hill preceded them along the sand-spit for the purpose of arranging with General Haggard for the joint advance on Chocolate Hill and Ismail Oglu Tepe. He met General Haggard, who pointed out that he was under General Sitwell's orders and could only act under instructions from that officer. He next met General Sitwell to whom he explained the orders he had received from General Hammersley.

General Sitwell replied that he had himself received different orders from General Hammersley and, according to General Hill's account, that it was impossible for him to co-operate in the proposed advance on Chocolate Hill and Ismail Oglu Tepe. General Sitwell, however, states that he informed General Hill that he could only spare two battalions out of the 32nd and 34th Brigades in support of General Hill's three battalions. Be this as it may, General Hill, believing that he could get no support from General Sitwell, decided to return to General Hammersley's headquarters at Lala Baba and report the situation. About this time General Haggard was severely wounded and General Sitwell for the time being assumed the direct command of the 32nd Brigade in addition to that of the 34th Brigade. After General Hill had left, General Sitwell detailed two battalions of the 32nd Brigade and one battalion of the 34th Brigade to be in readiness to support General Hill's battalions as soon as they came up.

On his way back to divisional headquarters General Hill met his three battalions advancing along the sand-spit north of Lala Baba and ordered them to halt and await further orders. On reaching headquarters he found that General Hammersley was away, but a General Staff Officer of the division informed him that the instructions previously given him by General Hammersley were correct, and that General Sitwell would be so informed. General Hill thereupon returned to his troops and again set them in motion towards and across the Cut and thence to the east of Hill 10, with a view to an advance on Chocolate Hill. This was about 12.45 pm. General Hill did not personally accompany his first three battalions, but followed with his two remaining battalions which by that time had landed and were concentrating near Lala Baba.

On arrival in the vicinity of Hill 10 at about 2.45 pm, General Hill found that his three leading battalions had circled round the north-east corner of the Salt Lake and were ready to move on Chocolate Hill, but that no battalions of the 32nd or 34th Brigade had been sent to co-operate on his left towards Ismail

Oglu Tepe. At 3 pm he telephoned to divisional headquarters to that effect, adding that he had seen
General Sitwell, who told him that two battalions
would be sent forward.

Just before the despatch of this message an order,
timed 2.40 pm, was issued from divisional headquarters to the effect that the advance would be
suspended for the present and resumed at 5.30 pm.
Two battalions of the 33rd Brigade with the Brigade
Commander, General Maxwell, would leave their
position near Lala Baba and move with their right
flank immediately north of the Salt Lake, so as to
come on the right of General Hill's troops. The general direction of the advance was to be on Chocolate
Hill. The advance was to be supported by all the
troops of the 32nd and 34th Brigades who had not
suffered heavy casualties. General Sitwell was to command the attack, and these brigades, as well as the
troops under General Hill, would act under General
Sitwell's orders. The divisional artillery near Lala Baba
would cover the attack, their fire beginning at 5.15
pm. This order, which was addressed to the 31st, 32nd
and 34th Brigades, reached General Hill shortly after
3.15 pm, and was no doubt received by General
Sitwell and General Maxwell at about the same time.
General Hill states that General Sitwell supported the
advance on the right flank with the two battalions of
the 33rd Brigade under General Maxwell at about 4
pm and that the 32nd and 34th Brigades took no part
in the attack on Chocolate Hill and Hill 70. On the
other hand, General Sitwell states that one battalion

of the 32nd Brigade and one battalion of the 34th Brigade followed General Hill's troops in support and a second battalion of the 32nd Brigade in reserve, and that he saw these three battalions engaged with the enemy. General Maxwell states that two battalions of the 34th Brigade operated on the left of General Hill's troops. The advance began somewhat earlier than had been ordered, but the artillery opened fire at the prescribed time, 5.15 pm. Chocolate Hill was captured, but no attempt was made to attack Ismail Oglu Tepe. It is not clear at what time and by what troops the capture of Chocolate Hill was effected. In the War Diary of the 31st Brigade it is recorded that Chocolate Hill was in the possession of that brigade at 5.30 pm, while General Hill, who commanded the brigade, states that Chocolate Hill was taken about dusk, and that in his opinion there was no reason why Ismail Oglu Tepe should not have been taken also, had the available battalions of the 32nd and 34th Brigades advanced more promptly on his left. He describes the Turkish opposition as not being very formidable. General Maxwell, who commanded the 33rd Brigade, ascribes the capture of Chocolate Hill solely to the action of his two battalions, and gives the time of its being taken as 7.20 pm. General Sitwell states that he was in telephonic communication with one of the two battalions of the 33rd Brigade, which reported at 11.30 pm that Chocolate Hill had been carried at 9.30 pm.

None of the three Brigadier-Generals concerned in the attack on Chocolate Hill—Generals Sitwell,

Hill and Maxwell—accompanied the troops. They established their report centres to the south of Hill 10, about two miles distant from Chocolate Hill, and remained there. In view of the distance and the nature of the country they can have seen but little of what was going on, and though no doubt they may occasionally have been in telephonic communication with some of their battalion commanders, the latter's outlook was limited and their responsibility was confined to what concerned their respective battalions. In the absence of superior military control and guidance on the spot, a force of inexperienced troops, unacquainted with local conditions and consisting of a number of battalions drawn from five brigades— namely, two from the 30th, three from the 31st, two from the 32nd, two from the 33rd and one from the 34th—must have been lacking in cohesion and cooperation, and the evidence discloses the confusion and delay which resulted from this cause.

Apparently Brigadier-Generals Sitwell, Hill, and Maxwell remained near each other at their several report centres until just before midnight on August 7th. General Sitwell then decided that General Hill should proceed to Chocolate Hill in order personally to ascertain the situation, and the latter set out at the time mentioned. On his own initiative General Sitwell directed General Hill to send back the following battalions which had been employed in the attack on Chocolate Hill with a view to their rejoining their respective brigades: the two battalions of the 32nd Brigade to the sand dunes south of Hill 10; the two battalions of the 33rd Brigade to Lala Baba; and the one battalion of the 34th Brigade to the brigade reserve south of Hill 10. At 7.30 am on August 8th General Hammersley visited General Sitwell at the latter's report centre, informed him that there was no enemy in the direction of Baka Baba, and suggested his joining General Hill on Chocolate Hill. The suggestion, however, was not pressed, and General Sitwell remained where he was.

It may here be mentioned that in his account of the attack on Chocolate Hill, which differs in some respects from the accounts of the three brigade commanders concerned, General Hammersley states that when he issued his order for the attack at 2.40 pm on August 7th, it was his intention that Ismail Oglu Tepe as well as Chocolate Hill should be captured, though no reference was made in the order to the former objective. He also states that the battalion of the 34th Brigade which took part in the operation was seriously engaged and its commanding officer severely wounded; that Chocolate Hill was captured by 7.30 pm; that up to 700 yards from the Turkish position all the fighting was done by General Hill's troops; and that in the final stage of the attack the two battalions of the 33rd Brigade advanced with great steadiness.

On August 7th Sir Frederick Stopford remained with Admiral Christian on board the *Jonquil*, where he considered himself to be in the best position to communicate with General Headquarters and with his subordinate commanders on shore.

OPERATIONS ON AUGUST 8TH

The distribution of the troops of the 11th Division on the morning of August 8th is described by General Hammersley as follows. One field battery and two mountain batteries were at Lala Baba. The 32nd Brigade was concentrated near Hill 10, except a detachment of two companies on the southern slopes of Kiretch Tepe Sirt. Two battalions of the 33rd Brigade were south of the Salt Lake and two at Lala Baba. Two battalions of the 34th Brigade were near Hill 10, one battalion was east of Hill 10, and one (the 11th Manchester Regiment) was on Kiretch Tepe Sirt. The divisional Pioneer Battalion (6th East Yorkshire Regiment) was at Lala Baba.

At this time the five Irish battalions under General Hill, which had been left in their advanced position when the other troops were withdrawn to the neighbourhood of the beach, appear to have been still holding Chocolate Hill and the ground in its vicinity.

The troops generally were much exhausted by the heat, thirst, and fighting of the previous day, besides which many men and parties were scattered owing partly to the mixing up of brigades and units in the attack on Chocolate Hill, and partly to straying in search of water, carrying and accompanying the wounded to the rear, and so on. We have, in fact, reason to believe that a considerable number of stragglers had collected at or near the shore.

The following movements took place on August 8th. One battalion of the 32nd Brigade, the 6th

Yorkshire Regiment, owing to the losses which it had sustained, was replaced by the divisional Pioneer Battalion, the 6th East Yorkshire Regiment, and this brigade under the command of Colonel Minogue was ordered to take up a line running north and south through Sulajik, so as to get in touch on the north with a battalion of the 34th Brigade (the 5th Dorset Regiment), and on the south with the troops under General Hill. In the course of the afternoon, Hill 70 was occupied by the Pioneer Battalion, and the huts at Sulajik were put in a state of defence, with trenches surrounding them, by the 67th Field Company, RE.

The 5th Dorset Regiment and the 9th Lancashire Fusiliers, also belonging to the 34th Brigade, were put under the orders of Sir Bryan Mahon, and so remained until August 12th, when they rejoined the 11th Division.

The 11th Manchester Regiment of the 34th Brigade, which on the 7th was acting under Sir Bryan Mahon, rejoined its brigade from Kiretch Tepe Sirt.

The 7th South Staffordshire Regiment of the 33rd Brigade was sent to reinforce the troops under General Hill.

On August 8th, Sir Frederick Stopford had been anxious to push on, and had informed his two divisional commanders that he regarded it as being of the greatest importance to forestall the enemy on the high ground north of Anafarta Sagir and on the sp running thence to Ismail Oglu Tepe. The divisional commanders, however, represented that, though they would do what they could, they doubted the possibility of a further advance on that day, the troops being much exhausted by continuous fighting and lack of water. Sir Frederick Stopford was also influenced by the fact that the artillery at his disposal consisted of only one field battery and two mountain batteries, and that the troops of the 10th and 11th Divisions had been much scattered in the operations of August 7th.

He decided therefore to postpone the attack on Ismail Oglu Tepe and the Anafarta Sagir ridge until dawn on the 9th. It was arranged to attack Ismail Oglu Tepe from Chocolate Hill and the Anafarta Sagir ridge from the north-west between Baka Baba and Chocolate Hill, the 33rd Brigade with one battalion of the 31st Brigade on the right, the 32nd Brigade on the left, and two battalions of the 34th Brigade in reserve. It appears from Sir Frederick Stopford's report to Sir Ian Hamilton of the operations of the IXth Corps, dated October 26th, 1915, that on August 8th the former informed his two divisional commanders that, in view of the inadequate artillery support, he did not want them to let their men make frontal attacks on entrenched positions, but they were to push on as far as possible and try to turn any trenches they came across.

In his despatch to the Secretary of State for War, dated December 11th, 1915, Sir Ian Hamilton drew special attention to this passage in Sir Frederick Stopford's report and paraphrased it as follows:

"General Stopford did not wish them to make frontal attacks on entrenched positions, but desired them, so far as was possible, to try and turn any trenches that were met with." He added: "Within the terms of this instruction lies the root of our failure to make use of the priceless daylight hours of August 8th." It is obvious that in one material respect the paraphrase differs from the instruction, which embodied three injunctions. First, to abstain from frontal attacks on entrenched positions; secondly, to push on as far as possible; and, thirdly, to try to turn any trenches which were encountered in pushing on. The second injunction is not mentioned by Sir Ian Hamilton, and the expression "as far as possible", which formed part of that injunction, is tacked on to the third.

Sir Ian Hamilton explains that in writing his despatch he had before him two documents from Sir Frederick Stopford—one, a memorandum to the Military Secretary, dated August 28th, written by Sir Frederick Stopford on board ship after he had been relieved of his command; the other, the report sent to Sir Ian Hamilton himself by General Stopford, dated October 26th—and that he inadvertently took up the former instead of the latter and quoted from it this sentence, which occurs textually in it as quoted, without the addition of "push on as far as possible." But in the early part of the paragraph in which the sentence occurs there is emphatic mention that Sir Frederick Stopford instructed his divisional generals to push on, and the sentence itself ends with a reiteration of the supreme importance of forestalling the enemy.

We think these facts show that there was some misunderstanding on the part of Sir Ian Hamilton as to the purport of the memorandum of August 28th and the report of October 26th, and we are of the opinion that his criticism is so worded as to obscure Sir Frederick Stopford's specific intention and injunction that the troops should push on as far as possible.

In the despatch Sir Ian Hamilton also referred to naval gunfire as compensating for the paucity of the available field and mountain artillery. Sir Frederick Stopford appears to have considered that, in the absence of a preparatory bombardment, the frontal attack of Turkish entrenchments would probably prove fruitless and entail heavy losses, and that as the trenches were not continuous the better course would be to push on between or past them, thus taking them in flank or reverse. As regards naval gunfire, Sir Frederick Stopford probably concurred with Admiral de Robeck in regarding such fire with its low trajectory as being ineffective against the deep trenches of the modern type, though effective enough against troops in the open or occupying shallow trenches. This view accords with much of the evidence which has been laid before us, while the importance of preparatory bombardment before making frontal attacks on deep entrenchments is confirmed not only by what repeatedly occurred on the Gallipoli Peninsula, but by the experience of our troops on the Western Front, where, the German trenches being continuous, attacks other than frontal are impossible.

Sir Ian Hamilton, who was at Imbros, received telegraphic reports of what was taking place at Suvla on August 7th from the commander of the IXth Corps. In particular there was a message despatched at 10 am on August 8th, reporting the position of the troops of the 11th Division at the time of despatch, and remarking that Major-General Hammersley and the force under his command deserved great credit for the results achieved. Presumably the capture of Chocolate Hill had been previously reported. The following message, despatched from Imbros at noon on August 8th, was sent by Sir Ian Hamilton to Sir Frederick Stopford:

> You and your troops have indeed done splendidly.
> Please tell Hammersley how much we hope from his
> able and rapid advance. Ian Hamilton.

With regard to this message, Sir Frederick Stopford informed us that the result of the operations on the night of the 6th and day of the 7th was not as satisfactory as he would have liked, but he gathered from Sir Ian Hamilton's congratulations that his dispositions and orders had met with the latter's approval.

Reverting to Sir Ian Hamilton's despatch of December 11th, 1915, we find it stated that the General Staff officer who had been sent from General Headquarters to Suvla early in the morning of the 8th reported by telegraph unfavourably as to the failure of our troops to take full advantage of the opportunities which were presenting themselves. But before this telegram was received, Sir Ian Hamilton had made up his mind from Sir Frederick Stopford's reports that all was not going well at Suvla, and he resolved himself to proceed thither, which he did, starting from Imbros at 4 pm and reaching Suvla an hour later. Sir Ian Hamilton's congratulatory telegram to Sir Frederick Stopford is hardly consistent with his conviction as recorded in the despatch, that all was not well at Suvla. It may, perhaps, have been written by Sir Ian Hamilton (as he said in his evidence) late on the 7th, or early on the 8th, as soon as the news of the capture of Chocolate Hill reached him; but if so we do not understand why its despatch from Imbros should have been delayed until noon on the 8th.

It is difficult to be certain as to the true explanation of this, but we do not consider the matter of great importance, as it is clear that for some reason Sir Ian Hamilton became dissatisfied on August 8th with the progress of operations, and consequently left Imbros for Suvla in the afternoon.

Sir Ian Hamilton's intervention

On arrival at Suvla Sir Ian Hamilton at once saw Sir Frederick Stopford on board HMS *Jonquil*, where, up to that time, the headquarters of the IXth Corps had been accommodated, pending their establishment on shore near Ghazi Baba. After a brief interview on the *Jonquil*, Sir Ian Hamilton's account of which is inconsistent with that of Sir Frederick Stopford, Sir Ian Hamilton proceeded to visit General Hammersley at Lala Baba. Sir Frederick Stopford did not accompany Sir Ian Hamilton to Lala Baba, and a good deal of conflicting evidence has been laid before us by these two officers with reference to his not doing so. The probable explanation of the incident is that Sir Frederick Stopford had only just returned from personally giving instructions to General Hammersley for the proposed operations at dawn on the 9th, and his attendance on shore not being requested by Sir Ian Hamilton, he saw no object in again visiting General Hammersley.

Sir Ian Hamilton arrived at Major-General Hammersley's headquarters about 6 pm, and in his despatch of December 11th, 1915, he describes the conversation which took place, and the extent to which he modified the orders previously given by Sir Frederick Stopford for the attack next morning. Sir Frederick Stopford and General Hammersley had decided against a night attack, but Sir Ian Hamilton thought that the advantages of such an attack in the matter of forestalling the enemy outweighed its disadvantages, and hearing that the 32nd Brigade was more or less concentrated and ready to move he gave General Hammersley a direct order that, even if it were only with this brigade, the advance should begin at the earliest possible moment instead of at dawn the next morning as previously arranged. Sir Ian Hamilton further directed that the 32nd Brigade should endeavour to occupy the heights north of Anafarta Sagir, presumably Tekke Tepe, but beyond giving these orders he states that he did nothing and said not a word calculated to affect the attack as originally planned. In his despatch he speaks of the 13 battalions detailed for the attack, but the correct number appears to be eleven, namely, four battalions of the 33rd Brigade, together with one from the 31st Brigade, on the right, with Ismail Oglu Tepe as the objective; four battalions of the 32nd Brigade on the left, with Anafarta Sagir as the objective; and two battalions of the 34th Brigade in reserve. It will be remembered that the remaining two battalions of the 34th Brigade had been placed at Sir Bryan Mahon's disposal on the morning of August 8th.

Sir Ian Hamilton's description of the nature and scope of his intervention is not fully corroborated by Sir Frederick Stopford and General Hammersley. Thus Sir Frederick Stopford points out in his report of October 26th, 1915, that his intention had been to make a concentrated attack upon the front stretching from Ismail Oglu Tepe to Anafarta Sagir, a distance of 4,100 yards, while under Sir Ian Hamilton's direct orders the front to be attacked was extended northward from Anafarta Sagir to Tekke Tepe, lengthening the front by an additional 2,200 yards. Moreover, the advance on this northern extension was through extremely difficult ground covered with dense bush, which had not been reconnoitred, and this greatly militated against the success of a night operation. Sir Frederick Stopford says in his report that, in view of the radical changes made by Sir Ian Hamilton in his plans and dispositions for the attack on the 9th, he repudiates any responsibility for the results of the action.

General Hammersley states that Sir Ian Hamilton's personal instructions quite upset the pre-arranged plans, and obliged him to re-issue his divisional orders late in the evening. Difficulty was experienced in communicating with the battalions of the 32nd Brigade, which were less concentrated than General Hammersley had supposed, and as a result only one battalion together with a section of engineers advanced in the direction of Tekke Tepe before 4 am on the 9th.

The change in the plan of operations approved by Sir Frederick Stopford was not communicated to him [Stopford] either by Sir Ian Hamilton or by General Hammersley. Sir Ian Hamilton states that he thought it would be reported by General Hammersley, and General Hammersley states that it did not occur to him at the time that he ought to report it. Later on, he imagines, the change was reported by some member of his staff to some member of the Corps staff. We think that this was an unfortunate omission. Sir Frederick Stopford might have expected to hear from the General Officer Commanding-in-Chief, and was entitled to hear from his divisional commander, in what respects his scheme of attack had been modified by direction of superior authority. If, however, Sir Frederick Stopford had accompanied Sir Ian Hamilton to Lala Baba, and been present at the latter's interview with General Hammersley, the alteration in the plan could not have been made without his knowledge.

At the end of the interview between Sir Ian Hamilton and Major-General Hammersley, the latter sent a General Staff officer to the commander of the 32nd Brigade with instructions to concentrate the brigade at Sulajik as soon as possible, and thence to occupy the high ground about Tekke Tepe before daybreak, at least one battalion being used for the purpose—preferably the 6th East Yorkshire Regiment. One battalion of the brigade was already at Sulajik; a second battalion reached that place without difficulty or delay; the third battalion, the 6th East Yorkshire Regiment, only got its orders to move from Hill 70 to Sulajik at 11 pm, and did not arrive until 3 am on the 9th; while the fourth battalion, the 9th West Yorkshire Regiment, had got out of touch in the thick bush near Abrikja at nightfall, never received the order to concentrate, and remained where it was.

OPERATIONS ON AUGUST 9TH

At 3.30 am on the 9th the brigade commander sent on the 6th East Yorkshire Regiment with the 67th Field Company, Royal Engineers (less one section), to secure Tekke Tepe, supporting the advance with another battalion, and retaining the third at Sulajik. On reaching a point about 1,000 yards south of Tekke Tepe, the head of the column was attacked by the Turks in superior strength; the commanding officers of the 6th East Yorkshire Regiment and the 67th Field Company, Royal Engineers, were killed; and many officers and men were killed or wounded.

Shortly afterwards two machine guns were lost. Meanwhile the battalion in support, pushing up on the left of the 6th East Yorkshire Regiment, lost its commanding officer and suffered heavy loss. Eventually the 6th East Yorkshire Regiment and the battalion supporting it, the 8th West Riding Regiment, fell back, and continued their retirement until about noon, when they reached a point about 1,000 yards westward of Sulajik near the north-east corner of the Salt Lake. Here General Sitwell with two battalions of the 34th Brigade had taken up his position at 6 am and this served as a rallying point for the two retreating battalions of the 32nd Brigade.

The battalion of the 32nd Brigade which remained at Sulajik was joined at daybreak by the 9th West Yorkshire Regiment, which during the night had got out of touch near Abrikja. At 8 am the Turks made a strong attack against our left at Sulajik which was held by these two battalions, and continued all day to press this attack, endeavouring to work round the left flank. Their attempts were repulsed.

It will be remembered that according to the original plan the attack on Ismail Oglu Tepe was to be carried out by the four battalions of the 33rd Brigade with one battalion of the 31st Brigade under General Maxwell. In General Hammersley's revised written orders, which were issued after the interview with Sir Ian Hamilton, certain changes were made. One battalion of the 33rd Brigade, the 9th Sherwood Foresters, was directed to take up the long line from Chocolate Hill to Damakjelik Bahr, so as to connect the extreme left of the Anzac troops with the force under General Hill. The 33rd Brigade being thus reduced to three battalions, General Hill was directed to place two instead of one of his five battalions at General Maxwell's disposal, and the objective of General Maxwell's force of five battalions was enlarged so as to include not only Ismail Oglu Tepe but the ridge running thence to Anafarta Sagir.

General Maxwell had reconnoitred the ground during the afternoon of the 8th, and observed that Hill 70 was occupied by the 6th East Yorkshire Regiment. He determined to place three of his battalions in the front line, with one battalion in support of the centre and one in reserve. About 4.45 am on August 9th the battalions were concentrated, and moved off to their several points of deployment. As soon as this movement began, a heavy rifle fire broke out from the direction of Abrikja, and Chocolate Hill was shelled by the enemy. The right and centre battalions, however, pushed on towards the ridge near Ismail Oglu Tepe. The left battalion, on approaching Hill 70, found it occupied by the Turks instead of our own men, the 6th East Yorkshire not having been replaced when ordered away the previous evening. In aggravation of this mishap a considerable Turkish force from the northeast attacked the battalion at close quarters. From Hill 70 the centre battalion was taken in enfilade [from end to end], and lost heavily. General Maxwell's advance was brought to a standstill and his left seriously threatened. It now became a question not of pushing the attack, but of holding on at all costs.

MOVEMENTS OF THE 53RD DIVISION

A reference must now be made to the 53rd Division,
under the command of Major-General Lindley, which
on arrival at Mudros had been kept there as a general
reserve for the combined operations which began on
August 6th. This division was ordered to Suvla on
August 8th. It consisted of three brigades—the 158th
under Brigadier-General Cowans, the 159th under
Brigadier-General Lloyd, and the 160th under
Brigadier-General Hume. It had no artillery, only one
Field Company of Royal Engineers without any
stores, and only one field ambulance. The divisional
Signal Company did not arrive until five or six days
after the landing of its division, and when it did arrive
it was attached to another division. The headquarters
of the division with one battalion of the 159th Brigade
were the first to arrive at Suvla, and landed at 7 pm on
the 8th. The rest of the division landed during the
night of the 8th and morning of the 9th. At 8.30 pm
on the 8th Major-General Lindley received orders that
two of his brigades, less one battalion for beach duty,
were to be attached to the 11th Division for operations
under General Hammersley on the following day. As
soon as the troops became available they were pushed
forward in the following order:

At 7 am [August 9th] one battalion, 160th
Brigade, in support of the 33rd Brigade near
Chocolate Hill.

At 9 am two battalions, 159th Brigade, to report
to General Sitwell at Hill 10.

At 9.20 am one battalion, 160th Brigade, to reinforce the battalion already sent to Chocolate Hill.

At 10.55 am the remaining two battalions, 159th Brigade, under General Lloyd, to report to General Sitwell at Hill 10.

At 6.35 pm one battalion of the 158th Brigade, the 1/1 Hereford Regiment, to strengthen the right flank of the 9th Sherwood Foresters, who had been pushed back with heavy loss to a position between Kazlar Chair and Hetman Chair.

After the reinforcements from the 53rd Division had joined the troops already in action the fight continued in a somewhat desultory fashion during the rest of the day, no serious reverse being sustained and no appreciable success being achieved. In the afternoon the bush caught fire behind three battalions under General Maxwell's command near Hill 70, and these battalions had to fall back towards Hill 50 and Sulajik.

DISTRIBUTION OF TROOPS ON THE EVENING OF AUGUST 9TH

At nightfall on the 9th the distribution of the troops was as follows:

The 9th Sherwood Foresters and 1/1 Hereford Regiment were near Hetman Chair.

Five battalions of the 10th Division under General Hill, with one field and one mountain battery, were on Chocolate Hill and Hill 50.

The 33rd Brigade, less the 9th Sherwood Foresters, plus two battalions of the 160th Brigade, under General Maxwell, were positioned from Hill 50 to the vicinity of Sulajik.

The 32nd Brigade, less one battalion, plus two battalions of the 159th Brigade, were at and to the north of Sulajik.

Two battalions of the 34th Brigade, with one battalion of the 32nd Brigade, were further to the north.

The remaining two battalions of the 34th Brigade were at Point 28, west of Kuchuk Anafarta Ova under the orders of the General Officer Commanding the 10th Division.

Two battalions of the 159th Brigade, presumably under General Lloyd, were near the north-east corner of the Salt Lake.

The 6th East Yorkshire Regiment (the Pioneer Battalion of the 11th Division), two field batteries and one mountain battery, were at Lala Baba.

It will be observed that the units were as much mixed up on the evening of August 9th as they had been on the previous evening, and organisation by brigades was practically non-existent. It would also appear that in the plan of operations for August 9th, which was initiated by Sir Frederick Stopford, more or less modified by Sir Ian Hamilton, and finally elaborated by General Hammersley, no reference was made to the troops of the 53rd Division, nor was any specific place or duty assigned to them. Yet presumably it must have been anticipated by each of these officers that the 53rd Division, or part of it, would have landed by the morning of the 9th, because General Lindley, who was the first to land, got an order from the IXth Corps at 8.30 pm on the 8th that he was to place two of his brigades, less one battalion, at General Hammersley's disposal for the operations on the 9th. Uncertainty as to the exact time of their landing may perhaps have led to the exclusion of these seven battalions from the plan of operations for August 9th, while the unfortunate repulse on both flanks on the morning of that day caused them to be hurried to the scene of action as soon as they could be got ready. They were much scattered in consequence, and removed from the control of their own divisional and brigade organisations, and this cannot have contributed to their fighting efficiency, especially as hardly any of their officers had been trained in the regular army or possessed previous war experience.

Position of the 10th Division

On August 8th and 9th Sir Bryan Mahon, commanding the 10th Division, but having with him of his own troops only two battalions of the 30th Brigade, one of the 31st Brigade, and his divisional Pioneer Battalion, supported by two battalions of the 34th Brigade which had been put under his orders, continued to push forward along Karakol Dagh and Kiretch Tepe Sirt, and entrenched a north and south line through a point marked on the map by a bench mark on the latter. Sir Frederick Stopford states that, taking into account the small force at his disposal and the lack of artillery support, the progress of Sir Bryan Mahon was as satisfactory as could be expected.

We think that it was unfortunate that the 10th Division had no opportunity of acting as a division under its own commander at the critical stages of these operations.

Orders from General Headquarters

Sir Ian Hamilton had spent the night of the 8th on board ship at Suvla and had watched General Hammersley's attack the next morning. After landing at Ghazi Baba at about 8 am he walked up the Karakol Dagh ridge as far as the headquarters of the 30th Brigade. He then appears to have returned to Imbros. At about 5 pm on the 9th Sir Frederick Stopford received a letter from General Braithwaite expressing the confident opinion that, if an attack of six or eight battalions could be organised under the command of a selected officer, and directed on Ismail Oglu Tepe and the ridge thence to Anafarta Sagir, the troops would attain their objective. The letter laid stress on the need for Sir Frederick Stopford's personal influence and driving power to get the operation driven through.

Sir Frederick Stopford regarded this letter as tantamount to an order from the General Officer Commanding-in-Chief. At the same time he was aware that the troops of the 11th Division and the seven battalions of the 53rd Division had lost heavily during the day's fighting and were considerably disorganised. There was, however, one brigade of the 53rd Division in reserve at Lala Baba which had not been engaged. Sir Frederick Stopford determined, therefore, to make the attack not with six or eight battalions only, as suggested in General Braithwaite's letter, but with the whole of the 53rd Division, less one battalion which had not yet landed, supported by the whole of the 11th Division.

OPERATIONS FROM AUGUST 10TH TO AUGUST 15TH

At 7.50 pm on August 9th, General Lindley received his orders for the attack which was to take place at 5 am on the following day. He found great difficulty in collecting his scattered battalions. In fact, two battalions of the 160th Brigade seem to have remained with the 33rd Brigade near Hill 50. There were three battalions of the Royal Welsh Fusiliers (158th Brigade) at Lala Baba, and these, with five other battalions (four of the 159th Brigade and one of the 160th Brigade), were eventually concentrated as two brigades near the position occupied by the 32nd Brigade at Sulajik. The right of this force moved south on Hill 70, but swung round to the west when about 200 yards from the top of the hill. It thus came under flank and reverse fire from the Turkish guns on Ismail Oglu Tepe and retreated, subsequently reforming behind the 33rd Brigade. The centre and left of the force were at first more successful, but by about 10.30 am the left was rapidly driven back, and with the retirement of the centre the attack came to an end. Under the orders of the Corps Commander the attack was renewed, after some artillery preparation, at 5 pm, but the opposition being greater than in the morning no headway was made, and the troops fell back to the alignment held the previous evening.

On August 10th Sir Frederick Stopford received orders from General Headquarters to take up and entrench a line across the whole front extending from Azmak Dere on the south through the knoll east of Chocolate Hill, to the ground held by the 10th Division on Kiretch Tepe Sirt. In giving effect to this order on August 11th he took the opportunity of reorganising his divisions and brigades. The entrenchment of the line from Kazlar Chair to 600 yards south of Sulajik was assigned to the 11th Division, thence to the west of Kuchuk Anafarta Ova to the 53rd Division, and thence to Kiretch Tepe Sirt to the 10th Division. The length of this line was over 5 miles.

During this day the 54th Division arrived at Suvla and began to disembark at Beach A. It had no artillery, no divisional signal company, no field ambulances, no ammunition, and no mules. The division was commanded by Major-General F. S. Inglefield, and consisted of the 161st Brigade under Brigadier-General Daniell, the 162nd Brigade under Brigadier-General De Winton, and the 163rd Brigade under Brigadier-General Brunker. Sir Frederick Stopford was directed not to employ the division without instructions from General Headquarters.

On the morning of August 12th General Stopford received orders from General Headquarters that the 54th Division was to make a night march that night and at dawn the next day to attack the heights of Kavak Tepe and Tekke Tepe and thence to Anafarta Sagir. The feasibility of a night march through an intricate and wooded country depends upon the absence of opposition along the route to be traversed, but in this case Sir Frederick Stopford had reason to believe that from Kuchuk Anafarta Ova eastward the ground was held by the enemy. He therefore decided to send forward the 163rd Brigade in the afternoon for the purpose of occupying Kuchuk Anafarta Ova and securing an unopposed night march for the remainder of the Division, at any rate as far as that place. In spite of serious opposition the 163rd Brigade succeeded in establishing itself at the desired point in very difficult and enclosed country. It was on this occasion that the officer commanding the 1/5th Norfolk Regiment with 16 officers and 250 men pursued the enemy into the forest, from which none of them ever emerged.

In the course of the same afternoon General Headquarters enquired whether Sir Frederick Stopford was satisfied that the 54th Division could be supplied with food, water, ammunition, etc., if the troops succeeded in gaining the high ground which was their objective. Sir Frederick Stopford replied that he foresaw grave difficulty in supplying the division, as in such difficult and densely wooded country the convoys would be attacked and the mules shot or stampeded. Thereupon the orders for the night march and the attack on the heights were cancelled by General Headquarters.

On August 13th Sir Ian Hamilton informed Sir Frederick Stopford that, as soon as Sir William Birdwood was ready to co-operate, a simultaneous attack was to be made by the latter on Sari Bahr and by the 11th and 54th Divisions on Ismail Oglu Tepe. Sir Frederick Stopford prepared plans accordingly. As it appeared, however, that Sir William Birdwood could not then undertake a fresh attack on Sari Bahr the project was abandoned, and Sir Frederick Stopford was directed to confine his attention to strengthening the entrenched line across his front.

To straighten out the left of this line Sir Frederick Stopford on August 14th directed Sir Bryan Mahon to advance on the following day and gain possession of the whole of the top of Kiretch Tepe Sirt. The 54th Division was ordered to co-operate. On the morning of the 15th the two brigades of the 10th Division, the 30th and 31st, made a frontal attack along the ridge, while the 162nd Brigade of the 54th Division supported on the right. Gunfire from two men-of-war in the Gulf of Saros and from one mountain battery, one field battery, and one heavy battery was brought to bear on the Turkish position. At first the attack succeeded and the top of the ridge was captured by the 6th Dublin Fusiliers. The Turks, however, made a counter-attack, and after severe fighting and heavy casualties our troops had to fall back to their original alignment.

THE RELIEF OF SIR FREDERICK STOPFORD

On the evening of August 15th Sir Frederick Stopford was relieved of the command of the IXth Corps and replaced for the time being by Major-General de Lisle. On his way from Cape Helles to Suvla, Major-General de Lisle had called at Imbros, seen Sir Ian Hamilton, and received formal instructions from Major-General Braithwaite. In these instructions he was informed that his immediate and most urgent concern was to reorganise the IXth Corps, and to prepare as large a proportion of it as possible for a fresh attack on Ismail Oglu Tepe, and the ridge running thence to Anafarta Sagir. The force placed at his disposal consisted of the 10th Division, less the 29th Brigade, the 11th, 53rd and 54th Divisions, and the 2nd Mounted Division, composed of about 4,000 dismounted men, which was expected to reach Suvla from Egypt by August 18th. As regards artillery, two mountain batteries, two heavy batteries and one field artillery brigade had been landed at Suvla. One field artillery brigade and two batteries of 5-inch howitzers had been landed at Anzac and were at the disposal of the General Officer commanding the IXth Corps as soon as horses could be provided to mobilise them. Three more field artillery brigades and two batteries of 4–5 inch howitzers were at Mudros, ready to be brought up as soon as they could be landed, but they would have to be landed without horses and taken into position by the horses of other units.

OPERATIONS ON AUGUST 21ST

On assuming command of the IXth Corps, Major-General de Lisle investigated the situation at Suvla and represented to General Headquarters the desirability of strengthening the force at his disposal by bringing over the 29th Division from Helles. This proposal commended itself to the General Officer Commanding-in-Chief and the 29th Division landed at Suvla on August 20th. The 2nd Mounted Division under Major-General Peyton had landed two days before. The attack was fixed for August 21st and Major-General de Lisle's plan, which met with Sir Ian Hamilton's approval, was as follows.

The 53rd and 54th Divisions were to hold the enemy from Sulajik to Kiretch Tepe Sirt; the 11th Division on the right and the 29th Division on the left were to attack Ismail Oglu Tepe and the ridge running thence to Anafarta Sagir; in support were to be the 2nd Mounted Division of Yeomanry, and in reserve were to be what remained of the two brigades of the 10th Division. It was arranged with Sir William Birdwood that a force of nine battalions should co-operate by advancing from Damakjelik Bahr so as to connect with the southern end of the outpost line of the IXth Corps near Kazlar Chair.

It had been decided to attack in the afternoon, and it so happened that a fog came on which seriously interfered with the preliminary bombardment of the enemy's position from 2.30 pm to 3 pm. The advance was begun at 3 pm by the 11th Division, the

34th Brigade rushing the Turkish trenches between Hetman Chair and Aire Kevak. In his despatch Sir Ian Hamilton states that this was done practically without loss, but Major-General Hammersley does not agree. He has informed us that one battalion lost five out of its seven officers before reaching the Turkish trenches and that by the end of the day the losses of this and of another battalion were extremely heavy.

The 32nd Brigade, moving directly against Hetman Chair and the communication trench thence eastward to Ismail Oglu Tepe, lost its proper direction by inclining too much to the north and came under a heavy enfilade fire. The brigade swung round to attack the communication trench from the north, but the attempt failed although successive lines advanced with conspicuous gallantry. Major-General Hammersley attributes this brigade's loss of direction to the fact that its right battalion lost all its officers within the first few hundred yards.

The 33rd Brigade, which was in divisional reserve, started from Lala Baba shortly after 3 pm towards Hetman Chair in support of the 34th and 32nd Brigades. During this movement some confusion arose from the 2nd Mounted Division, which was marching from Lala Baba to Chocolate Hill, cutting across the line of advance of the 33rd Brigade and temporarily separating the two battalions in front from the two battalions in the rear. The confusion was increased by a fierce bush fire which had started north of Hetman Chair. As a result the 33rd Brigade lost direction, part of it moving south-east towards

Susak Kuyu and part to the north of the Turkish communication trench. So far as the 11th Division was concerned the operation had failed.

Meanwhile at 3.30 pm, the 29th Division attacked Hill 70. The trenches on the hill were carried by the 87th Brigade on the left, but the 86th Brigade was brought to a standstill by the bush fire. Moreover its right was not supported owing to the 32nd Brigade having deviated from the proper direction. Later on the 86th Brigade fell back to a point south-west of Hill 70, where a little cover was obtainable, and eventually the division withdrew to its previous position.

Later on in the afternoon the 2nd South Midland Brigade of the 2nd Mounted Division was sent forward from its position behind Chocolate Hill in the hope that some substantial success might yet be achieved. The bush fire and the enemy's opposition retarded the brigade's advance and it was almost nightfall before it reached the valley between Hill 70 and Hill 100 on Ismail Oglu Tepe. A knoll near the centre of this valley was captured by one of the regiments of the brigade as soon as it was dark, but as this knoll was commanded by the enemy's trenches and could not be held in the day-time unless we were in possession of Ismail Oglu Tepe, the regiment and the brigade to which it belonged were ordered back to Chocolate Hill. It appears therefore that so far as the 29th Division and 2nd Mounted Division were concerned, the operation had failed.

The casualties in the IXth Corps on August 21st were approximately as follows: in the 11th Division,

58 out of 129 officers and 2,300 other ranks out of 6,400. In the 29th Division a little under 5,000 officers and men. In the 2nd Mounted Division which was about 4,000 strong, 1,200 officers and men, or 30 per cent.

The force under Major-General Cox, which had been detailed to co-operate with the IXth Corps on August 21st, advanced in three sections, the left to establish connection with the outpost line of the 11th Division near Kazlar Chair, the centre on Kabak Kuyu where there was a good supply of water, and the right on the Turkish trenches at Kaiajik Aghala. The advance of the left and central sections was successful. The right section met with obstinate resistance, but effected a lodgment on Kaiajik Aghala before nightfall and held on during the night against a superior force. The next morning an additional battalion reinforced this section, and after several attacks and counter-attacks a line from Kaiajik Aghala northward to Susak Kuyu was taken up and strengthened and subsequently connected with the right of the IXth Corps.

A FINAL OFFENSIVE ON AUGUST 27TH

On August 27th, Sir William Birdwood again detailed a force under Major-General Cox to complete the capture of Hill 60, immediately north of Kaiajik Aghala. The troops consisted of detachments from the 4th and 5th Australian Brigades, the New Zealand Mounted Rifles Brigade, and the 5th Connaught

Rangers. The advance was made at 5 pm and after severe fighting lasting through the night, the next day, and up to 1 am, on August 29th, the hill was captured. Our casualties on this occasion amounted to 1,000.

This was the last engagement of any serious importance at or in the vicinity of Suvla up to its evacuation.

CHANGE IN COMMAND AT SUVLA

We have already mentioned that Sir Frederick Stopford vacated the command of the IXth Corps on August 15th. Major-General Lindley resigned the command of the 53rd Division on August 17th. On August 18th Brigadier-General Sitwell was relieved of the command of the 34th Brigade on account of an adverse report on his capacity for command by Major-General Hammersley. Under orders from the War Office Major-General Hammersley was relieved of the command of the 11th Division on August 23rd. He received at the time a telegram from General Headquarters to the effect that no communication on the subject of his relief had emanated from Sir Ian Hamilton, but that presumably the War Office considered his age a bar. Major-General Hammersley was then nearly 57. On August 24th Major-General de Lisle vacated the temporary command of the IXth Corps and reverted to the command of the 29th Division, being replaced by Lieutenant-General the Hon. J. Byng. The reason for Lord Kitchener's action in regard to Sir Frederick Stopford and Major-General Hammersley appears to be as follows.

In a telegram to Lord Kitchener, dated August 14th, Sir Ian Hamilton reported that the result of his visit to the IXth Corps had bitterly disappointed him. He remarked:

> There is nothing for it but to allow them [the troops at Suvla] time to rest and re-organize, unless I force Stopford and his Divisional Commanders to undertake a general action, for which, in their present frame of mind, they have no heart. In fact, they are not fit for it.

Lord Kitchener replied on the same date, enquiring whether Sir Ian Hamilton had any competent generals to take the place of Sir Frederick Stopford, Sir Bryan Mahon and Major-General Hammersley. He added:

From your report I think Stopford should come home. This is a young man's war, and we must have commanding officers who will take full advantage of opportunities which occur but seldom. If, therefore, any Generals fail, do not hesitate to act promptly. Any Generals I have available I will send you.

Sir Ian Hamilton answered the foregoing telegram on the same date to the effect that the one man on the spot who could pull the IXth Corps together again was Major-General de Lisle. He remarked:

Unfortunately Mahon is senior to de Lisle, but I could not put him in command of the Corps at present, though as Divisional General he has done better than others, and I would ask him to accept the position ... I hope you will agree to this and give de Lisle the temporary rank of Lieutenant-General.

Lord Kitchener again telegraphed on the same date to the effect that he was asking Sir John French to supply one Corps Commander and two Divisional Generals, and had suggested the name of Lieutenant-General Byng for the Corps Command, and that it was better not to act definitely until he had heard what Sir John French could do.

It will be observed that this telegraphic correspondence between Sir Ian Hamilton and Lord Kitchener hardly bears out the telegram received by Major-General Hammersley from General Headquarters when he was relieved of his Divisional Command.

Sir Ian Hamilton has urged us to investigate and express our opinion on certain incidents which occurred in connection with Sir Frederick Stopford's removal from his command.

Sir Frederick Stopford was replaced by Major-General de Lisle on August 15th, and left forthwith for England. He thereupon ceased to be under Sir Ian Hamilton's orders, and on his way home he wrote a memorandum, dated August 28th, in which he gave an account of the operations at Suvla from the landing up to the day of his departure. On reaching London he forwarded this memorandum to the Military Secretary at the War Office for Lord Kitchener's information.

On August 14th the telegraphic correspondence mentioned in the preceding paragraph had taken place between Sir Ian Hamilton and Lord Kitchener. This was followed by a telegram from Sir Ian Hamilton, dated August 17th, in which the operations at Anzac and Suvla were described and commented on. A telegram, dated August 22nd, was then sent by Lord Kitchener to Sir Ian Hamilton, desiring him to transmit the operation orders and other instructions relating to the Suvla operations; and Sir Ian Hamilton replied on the same date that these documents had been forwarded by the last King's Messenger, who had left three days before.

On receipt of the documents a synopsis was prepared, and Lord Kitchener decided to assemble a Committee of senior General Officers at the War Office for the purpose of considering them, together with Sir Ian Hamilton's telegrams of August 14th and 17th and Sir Frederick Stopford's memorandum.

A copy of the memorandum was forwarded by the War Office to Sir Ian Hamilton on his return to England, and he does not appear to have taken exception to it at that time.

We understand Sir Ian Hamilton's present contention to be that Sir Frederick Stopford was not entitled to forward the memorandum of August 28th to the Military Secretary, except through himself as General Officer Commanding-in-Chief of the Mediterranean Expeditionary Force; and that the memorandum, being an irregular and *ex parte* [biased] statement, should have been debarred from consideration until he had been furnished with a copy and given an opportunity of expressing his views thereon.

The question raised by Sir Ian Hamilton being one of military discipline, and of administrative action on the part of Lord Kitchener as Secretary of State for War, its consideration appears to us to lie outside the scope of our enquiry.

REASONS FOR FAILURE AT SUVLA

Sir Beauvoir de Lisle attributes the failure on August 21st chiefly to the want of artillery. He states that there was not as much artillery on shore at Suvla as is normally assigned to a single division. About three-quarters of the artillery of one division had to support the attack of three divisions. Secondly, he is of the opinion that the troops landed at Suvla before the date of his assuming command of the IXth Corps had gone through a very trying experience, and that hardship, heat and thirst, coupled with futile attacks and repeated failures, had for the time being worn them out, shaken their self-reliance, and dulled their fighting spirit. Thirdly, he considers that the staff work generally had been indifferent and that consequently the troops had suffered more than they ought to have done.

Sir Beauvoir de Lisle gives no specific instance of this indifferent staff work as coming under his own observation, while he speaks in high terms of the professional qualifications of the Brigadier-General, General Staff, of the IXth Corps, Brigadier-General Reed, VC. He had no confidence in the fitness of Major-Generals Lindley and Hammersley for divisional commands in the field, and he thought that Major-General F. S. Inglefield, who at the time was 60, was too old for the command of the 54th Division. He was in favour of the evacuation of Suvla, which he regarded as the only thing to do when we had the factor of surprise no longer in our favour, and for the same reason he would have evacuated Helles and Anzac and abandoned the enterprise in June, as by that time there was no prospect of ultimate success. He described the operations planned by him for August 21st as having a defensive rather than an offensive object. He attacked in order to prevent the Turks from attacking.

POOR STAFF WORK

Sir Beauvoir de Lisle has spoken of the staff work in the IXth Corps as not being up to the proper standard, and certain incidents have come to our notice which support this allegation. General Hammersley put forward in his evidence a *précis* of the more important messages received at and issued from the headquarters of the 11th Division at Lala Baba, from 5 am to 5.40 pm, on August 7th. A message was sent by General Sitwell at 6.30 am that his troops were unable to move eastward from the vicinity of Hill 10, the order having been that they should so move for the capture of Chocolate Hill. To this message no reply was sent, but at 8 am another order was issued to General Sitwell that his troops and those of the 32nd Brigade were to advance on Chocolate Hill, supported on the left by the force under General Hill, which was to advance on Ismail Oglu Tepe.

At about the same time General Hill was told by General Hammersley that, when he reached the 32nd and 34th Brigades in the vicinity of Hill 10, he with the five battalions under his command was to operate on the right towards Chocolate Hill, the battalions of the 32nd and 34th Brigades operating on the left towards Ismail Oglu Tepe. Up to this time General Sitwell had shown no inclination to move forward, and the discrepancy between these orders, so far as concerned the tasks assigned to the several brigades, led to his neither taking action himself nor co-operating with General Hill. Again, when the final order for the combined attack on Chocolate Hill under General Sitwell's command was issued at 2.40 pm, no mention was made in it of Ismail Oglu Tepe as one of the objectives, though General Hammersley has informed us that he intended an attack on Ismail Oglu Tepe to form part of the operation. So far as we can judge, the orders emanating from General Hammersley's headquarters on August 7th were lacking in coherence and precision.

The unfortunate incident of the withdrawal of the 6th East Yorkshire Regiment from Hill 70 on the evening of August 8th, without its being replaced, also appears to indicate defective staff work. General Hammersley's account of this incident is far from clear. He tells us that he sent the 7th South Staffordshire Regiment belonging to the 33rd Brigade to reinforce General Hill at Chocolate Hill on the morning of the 8th, that General Hill ordered it forward at noon with directions to picket Hill 70 and entrench, but that Hill 70 was already occupied by the 6th East Yorkshire Regiment. Later on he tells us that the latter regiment advanced, under considerable fire, to the western slopes of Hill 70, that the fire became so intense that the Commanding Officer resolved to wait until dusk before occupying the hill, and that after dusk the hill was carried, and the troops began to entrench themselves. Later on, he tells us that, after his interview with Sir Ian Hamilton, he sent instructions to the Officer Commanding the 32nd Brigade at Sulajik, nominating the 6th East Yorkshire Regiment for the advance by night to Tekke Tepe, because he thought the battalion in question had been the least used so far, and was therefore the freshest. The battalion got orders to move from Hill 70 to Sulajik at 11 pm and, owing to the darkness and thick bush, did not arrive there until 3 am. No battalion was directed to replace the 6th East Yorkshire Regiment on its vacating Hill 70, which the Turks promptly re-occupied. In our opinion, General Hammersley did not know on August 8th that Hill 70 had been occupied, though this must have been known to General Hill, and is stated in evidence to have been observed by General Maxwell when he reconnoitred the ground east of Chocolate Hill. It would seem that these subordinate commanders or their staff took no steps to acquaint the divisional commander or his staff with what had occurred in regard to Hill 70.

The failure to replace the 6th East Yorkshire Regiment when ordered from Hill 70 to Sulajik entailed many fruitless attempts to recapture the hill and much unnecessary loss of life.

LACK OF ARTILLERY

Again, it will be seen on reference to an earlier paragraph in this report that on July 29th the General Officer Commanding IXth Corps was led to expect that he would be supplied with a considerable force of artillery, including seven brigades of field artillery—namely, the three brigades belonging to the 10th Division, two out of the three brigades belonging to the 11th Division, and two out of the three brigades belonging to the 13th Division. Up to August 8th only one field battery was available at Suvla, from August 9th to August 15th only one brigade of field artillery was available, and for the operations of August 21st Major-General de Lisle states that he had at his disposal only about three-quarters of the artillery of a division to support the attack of three divisions.

We think that the absence of the artillery and horses available at Alexandria and Mudros must have materially contributed to the failure at Suvla.

SIR IAN HAMILTON'S INTERVENTION

We have already mentioned Sir Ian Hamilton's personal intervention on the afternoon of August 8th and the consequent alteration in the scheme of attack which Sir Frederick Stopford had previously decided on. We regard the intervention as well-intentioned but injudicious. In the modified scheme the scope of the operations was enlarged so as to include the high ground near Tekke Tepe, but the difficulties of reaching and holding this ground were not appreciated, and as a result the attack in that direction was repulsed with heavy loss. Moreover, the withdrawal of troops for the movement on Tekke Tepe prejudicially affected the attack on Ismail Oglu Tepe, which also failed. We cannot say whether the original scheme would have succeeded, but we think that it had more chance of success than the scheme which took its place.

The combined operations so carefully planned were a failure, and the losses incurred at Helles, Anzac, and Suvla had been extremely heavy. As regards Anzac, Sir Ian Hamilton remarks in his despatch:

The grand coup had not come off. The Narrows
were still out of sight, and beyond field-gun range.
But this was not the fault of Sir William Birdwood,
or any of the officers and men under his command.

As regards Suvla, he remarks that the units of the
10th and 11th Divisions had shown their mettle in
the act of landing, when they stormed Lala Baba,
when they tackled Chocolate Hill, and when they
drove the enemy from Hill 10. He continues:

Then had come hesitation. The advantage had not
been pressed. The senior commanders at Suvla had
had no personal experience of the new trench
warfare; of the Turkish methods; of the paramount
importance of time. Strong, clear leadership had not
been promptly enough applied.

He concludes by stating that for these reasons he
had replaced Sir Frederick Stopford by Major-
General de Lisle.

DIFFICULTIES OF HILL WARFARE

It must be remembered that a great part of the fighting at both Anzac and Suvla was not trench warfare,
but hill warfare. Hill warfare is not an easy business for
troops unaccustomed to it, even when the hills are
bare and the slopes normal, but its difficulties are
greatly increased when the hills are covered with forest or dense bush, and the slopes are precipitous. The

difficulties are further intensified if the operations are undertaken at night. Certain general principles for the guidance of commanders who may propose to undertake night operations have been authoritatively set forth in Field Service Regulations, 1914, Part I, Chapter IX, particular stress being laid on the importance of a complete preliminary reconnaissance. Local conditions at Anzac and Suvla did not allow the thorough reconnaissance prescribed in this chapter. Exceptional conditions may justify a departure from established tactical rules, and we do not doubt that Sir Ian Hamilton carefully balanced the advantages of surprise and immunity from hostile fire against the risk of misdirection, confusion, and delay. In the opinion of Sir William Birdwood and Sir Frederick Stopford night attacks were justified by the special circumstances. Still, having regard to the results, the history of the operations at Anzac and Suvla seems to us to substantiate the soundness of the regulations on this subject.

It may be mentioned, that in Lord Kitchener's telegram to Sir Ian Hamilton on April 2nd, Lord Kitchener had referred to night attacks without confessing any opinion thereon.

In his despatch, Sir Ian Hamilton describes Koja Chemen Tepe as the dominating point, the acquisition of which would necessarily lead to the capture of Maidos and Kaba Tepe, would enable the bulk of the Turkish Army to be cut off from land communication with Constantinople, and would give our artillery such a command as to stop all sea traffic between the

Turkish Army and Constantinople or Asia. We suggest that these objects would not have been attained without a protracted struggle, the result of which cannot confidently be predicted.

THE INTERIM DECISION TO CONTINUE OPERATIONS

After the failure at Suvla on August 6th and the following days, the same question presented itself to the Dardanelles Committee and the Cabinet as in May, i.e., whether the Dardanelles operations were to be continued or abandoned, and, if continued, in what way.

The question was raised in a memorandum prepared by Colonel Swinton, the Assistant-Secretary to the Committee of Imperial Defence, and laid before the meeting of the Dardanelles Committee on the 19th August, 1915:

> There appear to be only two alternative courses to be adopted:
>
> (*a*) Not to send out the additional troops asked for by the Commander-in-Chief, and, therefore, to abandon the attempt to force the Straits, for there appears to be no prospect of success in a further offensive if the troops out in Gallipoli are not so increased, and without advancing it appears to be impracticable to continue to occupy the portions of the peninsula already gained.
>
> (*b*) To send out the troops asked for and to despatch them with the least possible delay so that the attempt which has just failed may be renewed. These reinforcements should be sent out at the earliest possible moment in view of the broken weather to be expected in the last half of September, which will render landing and supply impossible for considerable periods.

This was not quite exhaustive, for it was possible to send out smaller reinforcements which would enable Sir Ian Hamilton to maintain his position till a final decision was reached, and this was the plan adopted.

The reinforcements asked for were those which had been mentioned by Sir Ian Hamilton in a telegram of August 17th in which he stated that the

Turks had 110,000 rifles on the peninsula to his 95,000; that his British divisions were 45,000 under establishment, exclusive of about 9,000 promised or on the way, and that he required—to give him the necessary superiority if the Turks were not largely reinforced—that this deficit should be made up and that new formations, totalling 50,000 rifles, should be sent.

The matter was discussed at many meetings of the Dardanelles Committee. Sir Ian Hamilton's views were considered, and appreciations were submitted by the General Staff, which had been reconstituted under Sir Archibald Murray, and afterwards under Sir William Robertson. The final decision was not reached until December, 1915.

The position when Sir Ian Hamilton's telegram of August 17th was received was broadly this. It had been agreed at a joint Conference between the French and British authorities held at Calais in July, 1915, that no important offensive should be undertaken in the West until the spring of 1916. This would reduce the demands from the Western Front for men and munitions and might make it possible to move troops thence to the East.

It had become clear that no help could be looked for from Bulgaria, and that that country had become definitely hostile, and would probably join the Central Powers, as in fact she did very soon. It was likely that if Bulgaria joined the Central Powers an attack would be made on Serbia with the object of crushing that country and opening up communication with Constantinople. If this were done, the Turks could be supplied with guns and ammunition which they were known to want. The Russian reverses were still continuing.

It seemed to be agreed that it would not be wise to abandon the operations in the Dardanelles unless some operations in the Balkans or other operations against Turkey in some direction were undertaken, and there was undoubtedly a difference of opinion as to the course to be adopted.

On August 20th, Lord Kitchener pointed out that, owing to the situation in Russia, he could no longer maintain the attitude which was agreed upon in conjunction with the French at Calais (in July), namely, that a real serious offensive on a large scale in the West should be postponed until all the Allies were quite ready; and that the large divisional reinforcements asked for could not be sent to the Dardanelles, as they had been promised to France and could not be diverted. He said his inclination was to help Sir Ian Hamilton as far as was possible without interfering with the operations in France, at any rate until after the contemplated offensive there had taken place.

This was agreed to, and Sir Ian Hamilton was so informed. He replied that he would do the best he could with the forces at his disposal; and after giving an account of some fighting that had taken place, and pointing out that casualties, both from wounds and sickness, were very large, he said:

> Keeping these conditions in view, it appears
> inevitable that within the next fortnight I shall be
> compelled to relinquish either Suvla Bay or Anzac
> Cove, and must further envisage the possibility of a
> still further reduction of my front in the near future.

Later on, he reported that if Suvla or Anzac had to be given up, he thought it must be Suvla.

In answer, Lord Kitchener desired him to discuss the matter with his Corps Commanders, and referred to 47,000 drafts and reinforcements which had been sent since August 6th.

Sir Ian Hamilton replied that he did not understand the allusion to 47,000, as he had not been advised of any such number, and, in answer, Lord Kitchener said that he was sending the details. On this, Sir Ian Hamilton telegraphed that the welcome news of 47,000 reinforcements altered the whole situation, and that such a number would do much to complete his diminished cadres [units], and should materially lessen the sickness rate by giving more chance of taking tired troops out of the trenches. In fact, Sir Ian Hamilton appears to have received reinforcements amounting to 29,000, but of these 9,000 were not sufficiently trained for active service and had to be sent to Egypt, reducing the effective total to 20,000.

On August 27th, the Dardanelles Committee, after discussion, decided that no line of future policy could be framed for the present, but that Sir Ian Hamilton should do his best to hold the ground which he had gained, and be asked for his appreciation as to future policy and the requirements to carry it out. On the same date Lord Kitchener telegraphed to Sir Ian Hamilton accordingly.

Sir Ian Hamilton's appreciation was sent on September 2nd, and in it he pointed out that the drafts and reinforcements promised did not make up his deficit, and that he could not launch any grand attack unless or until his divisions could be brought up to establishment and new formations up to 50,000 were sent out. He also asked for reinforcements up to 20 per cent to be available in the theatre of operations to meet wastage. He concluded:

> To sum up, there is, in my opinion, no better
> alternative than to make fresh effort at Suvla and
> Anzac. You will understand that any appreciation I
> can send must inevitably alter from day to day, and
> that it must be again modified by any accession to
> my strength in the shape of fresh Allied troops or an
> alteration in the political situation in the Balkans.
> Meanwhile, all preparations are being made for a
> winter campaign.

When this came before the Dardanelles Committee on September 3rd, they were informed by Lord Kitchener that the French Government had decided to send four divisions against Turkey to the Asiatic side of the Dardanelles and wished their two divisions on the European side to be replaced by British troops. Lord Kitchener said that he proposed to instruct Sir John French to send two divisions from France for the purpose. This enterprise, if carried out by the French, might have materially assisted the operations in the Dardanelles, and in any case was inconsistent with the abandonment of the Gallipoli Expedition.

Preparations were made for carrying out this scheme, but the French troops could not be sent from the Western Front until the result of the contemplated offensive in that theatre was known. This offensive began on September 25th, and in the meantime the Bulgarians had mobilized, and evidently an attack on Serbia was probable. Another element was thus introduced into the problem, namely, the consideration of whether an Allied force should be sent to Salonica or elsewhere to help the Serbians. On September 23rd the Secretary of State for War was directed to prepare a military appreciation of the situation to be placed before the Dardanelles Committee on the morning of September 24th on the following lines:

> The possibility of sending a British or Allied force to Salonica or farther in order to support Greece, if Greece should go to the assistance of Serbia in resisting an attack by the Austro-Germans and possibly the Bulgarians.

On September 24th Sir Ian Hamilton was asked what force could be spared from Gallipoli for Salonica. At the same time the attention of the Admiralty and War Office was to be drawn to the importance of pushing on arrangements for a winter campaign in the Gallipoli Peninsula.

The circumstances which led to the despatch of forces to Salonica do not come within the scope of our enquiry. It is sufficient to say that for a long time questions were raised and discussions took place about the matter, and eventually the British Government was committed to sending a large force to co-operate with the French in that theatre. The possibility of having to send this force again raised the question of the evacuation of Gallipoli.

There was a considerable division of opinion on the subject among the members of the Dardanelles Committee and, on October 11th, it was decided that immediate instructions should be given for the despatch, as soon as the pending operations on the Western Front were over, of an adequate force from France to Egypt, without prejudice to its ultimate destination, and that a specially selected General should proceed without delay to the Near East to consider and report as to the particular sphere and the particular objective to which we should direct our attention. Sir Charles Monro was the General selected, and he left England on October 22nd, and arrived at Gallipoli on October 31st.

THE DECISION TO EVACUATE

On October 14th the Government decided to recall Sir Ian Hamilton, and on October 20th General Sir Charles Monro was ordered to take over the command of the forces in the Mediterranean, and received written instructions from Lord Kitchener to report "fully and frankly" on the military position. He was instructed to consider the best means of removing the existing deadlock, and to report "whether, in his opinion, on purely military grounds, it was better to evacuate Gallipoli or to make another attempt to carry it." He was also asked to give his estimate of the loss which would be incurred in the course of an evacuation.

Sir Charles Monro left on October 22nd, arriving at Mudros on the 27th. After an inspection of the peninsula he came to the conclusion that the forces should be withdrawn. He never swerved from this opinion, which he communicated to Lord Kitchener in the following telegram on October 31st:

> With the exception of the Australian and New Zealand Army Corps the troops on the peninsula are not equal to a sustained effort, owing to inexperienced officers, the want of training of the men, and the depleted condition of many of the units.
>
> We merely hold the fringe of the shore, and are confronted by the Turks in very formidable entrenchments, with all advantages of position and power of observation of our movements. The beaches are exposed to observed artillery fire, and in the restricted areas all stores are equally exposed. We can no longer count upon any action by surprise as the Turks are in considerably stronger force than they were, and have had ample time to provide against surprise landings.
>
> Since the flanks of the Turks cannot be attacked, only a frontal attack is possible, and no room is afforded on any of the beaches for the distribution of additional divisions should they be sent, nor is there sufficient space for the deployment of an

adequate force of artillery, the action of which would be impaired by poverty of observation and good positions for searching or counter battery effects. Naval guns could only assist to a partial degree.

In fact an attack could only be prosecuted under the disadvantages of serious lack of depth, and of absence of power of surprise, seeing that our line is throughout dominated by the Turks' position. The uncertainty of weather might also seriously hinder the landing of reinforcements and regularity in providing the artillery ammunition to the amount which would be required.

It is therefore my opinion that another attempt to carry the Turkish lines would not offer any hope of success; the Turkish positions are being actively strengthened daily. Our information leads to the belief that heavy guns and ammunition are being sent to the peninsula from Constantinople. Consequently by the time fresh divisions, if available, could arrive, the task of breaking the Turkish line would be considerably more formidable than it is at present.

On purely military grounds, therefore, in consequence of the grave daily wastage of officers and men which occurs, and owing to the lack of prospect of being able to draw the Turks from their entrenched positions, I recommend the evacuation of the peninsula

After adding that he was unable at that moment to give any definite estimate of the losses which would be incurred in a withdrawal, Sir Charles Monro concluded his telegram by saying:

> I have endeavoured in the expression of my opinion to give full weight to the effect which will be created in the East by our evacuation, and I consider that the force now in the peninsula, or such portion of it as we may be able to evacuate, would be more favourably placed in Egypt. This force stands in need of rest, re-organisation, and especially of training, before it can be usefully employed. The Corps and Divisional Commanders have done splendid work in the peninsula, but they do not possess the opportunity or time, as they now stand, to create the force into a reliable fighting machine. Hence I think loss of prestige caused by withdrawal would be compensated for in a few months by increased efficiency.

Sir Charles Monro told us that his opinion was strengthened by the state of health of the troops. The rate of sickness had been alarmingly high in the hot months of August and September. On August 23rd Sir Ian Hamilton had reported to Lord Kitchener that the average net wastage, even when there were no serious engagements, amounted, owing to sickness, to 24 per cent a month. In September the medical officers had reported that 50 per cent of the men in seven battalions of the old troops examined at Anzac had feeble hearts with shortness of breath, that 78 per cent of these had diarrhoea, and 64 per cent had sores on the skin. On the first three days of October over 1,800 sick were evacuated from the IXth Corps at Suvla, and at times the number of such evacuations from Suvla, Anzac, and Cape Helles amounted to 1,000 a day. In August, September and October, the number of sick evacuated from the peninsula amounted to [★].

In addition the troops were continuously under fire, the beaches and rest trenches being shelled as much as the front lines. The men in reserve had to spend the night in getting up stores to the front and in making communications. Fatigue parties had to be constantly occupied in unloading the contents of the transports into lighters and from the lighters to the shore. Although there was a notable decline in the sick rate shortly after Sir Charles Monro's arrival, Sir William Birdwood on November 4th telegraphed to Lord Kitchener as follows:

> Byng and Davies and all their Divisional
> Commanders have very little faith in their troops'
> present power of endurance, and reply that with few
> exceptions none are at present capable of more than
> 24 hours of sustained offensive effort. The same
> applies to most of the Australians owing to amount of
> sickness we have had, from which they have by no
> means recovered.

On November 1st General Monro was asked by Lord Kitchener if his Corps Commanders were of the

★ Figure not available at the time the report was signed.

same opinion as himself. Sir Charles Monro accordingly consulted Sir William Birdwood, Sir Julian Byng and Sir Francis Davies, and asked them to submit their views in writing. He urged them "earnestly to give their opinions without paying any heed to his."

General Birdwood wrote:

> I agree with General Monro regarding the grave disadvantages of our position and the extreme difficulty of making any progress. But I consider that the Turks would look upon our evacuation as a complete victory. From Indian experience I fear the result on the Mahometan [Muslim] world in India, Egypt, Persia. I am therefore opposed to evacuation. I am of the opinion that, if we leave the peninsula, it is essential that the whole force must be launched immediately against the Turks elsewhere, and I fail to see where this can be done with confident hope of success. I am adverse to withdrawal which would enable Turkish forces to proceed to Caucasus or Mesopotamia; landing elsewhere than in Turkey would not have the same effect. I also fear that the morale effect on our troops of withdrawal would be bad, while the Turkish morale would proportionately rise. Season being so late and bad weather at hand, I think actual withdrawal fraught with difficulty and danger, as ample time and continuous fine weather essential. All embarkations must be done at night, and only four or five nights a week can now be counted on. Heavy loss might be caused by the advent of any continuous bad weather after withdrawal has been partially carried out.

General Byng replied:

> I consider evacuation desirable. As regards Suvla, a
> voluntary and not very costly retirement is feasible at
> the present time, but it seems possible that with
> German help to the enemy a compulsory and
> therefore costly retreat may be necessitated.

General Davies replied:

> I agree with General Monro.

The opinions of these three officers were then
fully communicated to Lord Kitchener by Sir Charles
Monro in a telegram on November 2nd, in which he
repeated his opinion as to the necessity of evacuating,
and as a "rough estimate" stated that Admiral de
Robeck and his Corps Commanders thought a loss
of 30 to 40 per cent in personnel and material might
be incurred, and that he was "inclined to agree with
their estimate".

Sir Charles Monro's opinion in favour of evacuation made it necessary for the authorities at home to
come to a decision of great gravity. On October 7th
the War Committee had replaced the Dardanelles
Committee, and on November 3rd both the War
Committee and the Cabinet invited Lord Kitchener
to go out to the Mediterranean in order to assist them
in arriving at a final decision.

On the same day Lord Kitchener telegraphed to
Sir William Birdwood:

Very secret.

You know the report sent in by Monro. I shall come out to you; am leaving tomorrow night. I have seen Captain Keyes, and I believe the Admiralty will agree to making naval attempt to force the passage of the Straits. We must do what we can to assist them, and I think that as soon as our ships are in the Sea of Marmora we should seize the Bulair isthmus and hold it so as to supply the Navy if the Turks still hold out.

Examine very carefully the best position for landing near the marsh at the head of the Gulf of Xeros, so that we could get a line across the isthmus, with ships at both sides. In order to find the troops for this undertaking we should have to reduce the numbers in the trenches to the lowest possible, and perhaps evacuate positions at Suvla. All the best fighting men that could be spared, including your boys from Anzac and everyone I can sweep up in Egypt, might be concentrated at Mudros ready for this enterprise.

There will probably be a change in the naval command, Wemyss being appointed in command to carry through the naval part of the work.

As regards the military command, you would have the whole force, and should carefully select your commanders and troops. I would suggest Maude, Fanshawe, Marshall, Peyton, Godley, Cox, leaving others to hold the lines. Please work out plans for this, or alternative plans as you may think best. We must do it right this time.

I absolutely refuse to sign orders for evacuation, which I think would be the gravest disaster and would condemn a large percentage of our men to death or imprisonment.

Monro will be appointed to the command of the Salonica force.

In order to explain the telegram quoted above, it is necessary to state that after the failure of the military operations in August, a section of responsible naval officers, foremost among whom were Admiral Wemyss and Sir John de Robeck's Chief of the Staff, Commodore Keyes, held very strongly that the fleet should renew the attempt to force the Straits in order to relieve the army. A plan of operations had been worked out, with the assent of Sir John de Robeck. It was thought by these officers that, if three or four battleships and six or eight destroyers could pass through the Straits, they would be able, in combination with the submarines, to dominate the Sea of Marmora, thus cutting the main Turkish lines of communication and supply, which ran from the Asiatic side of the peninsula.

Sir John de Robeck was not in favour of this project, which he thought underestimated the dangers and difficulties of the operation, and overrated the effect that a successful naval attack would produce. But he felt, nevertheless, that the contrary view should be fully put before the Admiralty, and towards the end of October he allowed Commodore Keyes to return home to do this. On arriving in England, Commodore Keyes discussed his plan of operations fully with Mr Balfour and the Sea Lords. He also had two interviews with Lord Kitchener on November 3rd and 4th. When he left for the Mediterranean on November 4th, Commodore Keyes told us he was under the impression that his suggestion had been regarded with favour.

Between November 3rd and 4th Lord Kitchener's proposal to seize the Bulair isthmus had been considered and adversely criticised by the Admiralty, by Sir William Birdwood, and by Commodore Keyes. On November 4th Lord Kitchener again telegraphed to Sir William Birdwood, intimating that a renewal of the naval attack might not be approved, and adding:

> I am coming as arranged, and shall be at Alexandria Monday night or Tuesday morning. Shall stay there one day without landing and without my presence being known. After seeing Maxwell and Macmahon, shall come on to you, leaving in the evening.
>
> The more I look at the problem the less I see my way through, so you had better very quietly and secretly work out any scheme for getting the troops off the peninsula.

Lord Kitchener left for the Mediterranean on the evening of November 4th. In the course of the following days he discussed the position with Sir John Maxwell, Sir Henry Macmahon and Sir Charles Monro, at Alexandria and Mudros. The telegrams which then passed between him and the Prime

Minister show that Lord Kitchener was greatly concerned as to the difficulty of defending Egypt, in the event of an evacuation of the peninsula; and that he advocated a landing at Ayas Bay, in the neighbourhood of Alexandretta, with the object of cutting the Turkish railway communications. This project necessitated the withdrawal of forces from both Salonica and France, and the diversion of Indian divisions then on their way to Mesopotamia. It did not commend itself to the General Staff at the War Office, and was ultimately rejected at a joint conference between representatives of the British and French Governments held at Paris on November 17th.

On November 15th Lord Kitchener reported to the Prime Minister the result of his personal inspection of the positions on the peninsula in the following telegram:

> To gain what we hold has been a most remarkable feat of arms. The country is much more difficult than I imagined, and the Turkish positions at Achi Baba and Kilid Bahr are natural fortresses of the most formidable nature, which, if not taken by surprise at first, could be held against very serious attack by larger forces than have been engaged, even if these forces had proper lines of communication to support them. This latter want is the main difficulty in carrying out successful operations on the peninsula.
>
> The landings are precarious and often impossible through rough sea and want of harbours, and the enemy's positions are peculiarly suitable for making

our communications more dangerous and difficult. The base at Mudros is too far detached from our forces in the field, and the proper co-ordination of the administrative services of a line of communications is prevented by distance and sea voyages dependable on the weather. This state of things, in my judgment, is the main cause of our troops not having been able to do better, and to attain really strategic points on the peninsula, which would have turned Kilid Bahr, and unless this were done I do not consider that the Fleet ever could have passed the Straits. Everyone has done wonders, both on sea and land, when the natural difficulties that have had to be surmounted are considered. Our present positions, in my opinion, can be held against the Turks even if they received increased ammunition.

The trenches have been well dug, and bomb-proof covering has been afforded for the men; supplies and water are on shore, and officers and men are confident that they can hold out against the Turks, but they are somewhat depressed at not being able to get through. I consider, however, the lines are not deep enough, if Germany sent a German force to attack, to allow proper arrangements for supports, and if the front line trenches were taken, these difficulties would increase. I consider that advances from our present positions are very difficult, particularly from Helles and Anzac. Suvla gives some opportunity for improving our positions, but it seems very doubtful whether this would enable us to push through.

About 125,000 Turks are immobilised by our occupation of the peninsula, and they are caused considerable loss, and, until the recent German operations in Serbia opened communications with Turkey and changed the situation, practically the whole Turkish Army had to be held in readiness to defend the capital if we succeeded on the peninsula. In present circumstances the *raison d'etre* of our forces on the Gallipoli Peninsula is no longer as important as it has been hitherto, and if another position in the neighbourhood of Alexandretta were occupied, where Turkish movements eastward could be effectively stopped, the realisation of the German objective against Egypt and the East would be prevented.

Careful and secret preparations for the evacuation of the peninsula are being made. If undertaken it would be an operation of extreme military difficulty and danger; but I have hopes that, given time and weather, which may be expected to be suitable until about the end of December, the troops will carry out this task with less loss than was previously estimated. My reason for this is that the distance they had to go to embark, and the contraction of the lines of defence to be held by a smaller force, gives them a better chance than I thought previously.

The Admiral and Generals Monro and Birdwood, to whom I have read the above, all agree.

Later in the same day Lord Kitchener telegraphed further to the Prime Minister that Admiral de

Robeck would like to retain Cape Helles, even if Suvla and Anzac were evacuated.

On November 19th the Prime Minister telegraphed to Lord Kitchener that:

His Majesty's Government had decided against the proposed expedition to Ayas Bay as a result of their conference in Paris with the French Government, and Naval and Military authorities, and after consideration of the maritime position in the Mediterranean

and requested Lord Kitchener to give his "considered opinion as to the evacuation of the peninsula, in whole or in part," on the basis of the Ayas Bay scheme having been withdrawn.

In reply, Lord Kitchener telegraphed on November 22nd to the effect that, while our offensive had up to the present held up the Turkish Army, German assistance was now practically available, that this assistance would make our positions untenable, and that evacuation, therefore, seemed inevitable. He therefore recommended that the evacuation of Suvla and Anzac should be proceeded with, while Cape Helles should be held for the present. The retention of Cape Helles would enable the Navy to maintain the advantages already gained, still threaten the seizure of the Straits, and also give greater facilities for the evacuation of Suvla and Anzac.

On November 23rd the War Committee came to the decision that:

Having regard to the opinions expressed by Lord Kitchener in his telegram dated November 22nd, 1915, and by the General Staff in their memorandum dated November 22nd, 1915, the War Committee feel bound to advise the evacuation of the Gallipoli Peninsula on military grounds, notwithstanding the grave political disadvantages which may result from the decision. They have carefully examined the naval considerations in favour of the retention of Cape Helles as stated in a note by the Chief of the Admiralty War Staff, printed with the General Staff Memorandum referred to above. They are of the opinion, however, that the naval advantages to be gained by this course are not commensurate with the military disadvantages involved.

The proposal to evacuate was then discussed at a Cabinet Council on the following day. At this Council Lord Curzon told us that he "and several of his colleagues, anxious at least that the opposite side should be heard, and fearful of a decision fraught with such fearful possibilities, pleaded for a few hours' consideration", and that he "undertook to state the case to the best of his ability".

The case against evacuation was then elaborated by Lord Curzon in two memoranda dated November 25th and 30th, in which the military and political reasons in favour of and against evacuation were fully discussed. Lord Curzon's arguments were replied to by Mr Bonar Law in a memorandum circulated on December 4th, which ended as follows:

So far I have considered the question from a military point of view, and my conclusions may be disputed, but there is another aspect of it which is not military, and which is not open to dispute. Recognising the seriousness of the position at the Dardanelles, the Government decided to send a military expert to report on the question of evacuation. For this purpose Sir Charles Monro was chosen. On the 31st October he reported in the strongest possible terms in favour of evacuation. He sent us also the opinions of three of the Generals on the spot—Generals Birdwood, Byng and Davies. Of these three General Birdwood alone was opposed to evacuation, but the reasons given by him for his opposition were entirely political, and he agreed with General Monro regarding the 'great disadvantages of our position and extreme difficulty of making any progress.' Afterwards he concurred in a telegram sent by Lord Kitchener on the 22nd November which contained these words: 'Our offensive on the peninsula has, up to the present, held up the Turkish Army, but with German assistance, which is now practically available, our positions there cannot be maintained, and evacuation seems inevitable.' Not satisfied with General Monro's report, the Government decided to send Lord Kitchener. In a telegram sent from Paris, on his way, Lord Kitchener showed clearly that he was entirely opposed to evacuation, and he has since told us that he held that view when he started for the Dardanelles. The actual examination of the situation, on the spot, however, changed his opinion, and he telegraphed to the Prime Minister in favour of evacuation in words which I have just quoted. We also consulted our General Staff on the subject. They gave us an opinion as definite as that of the other Generals in favour of evacuation. It is the fact, therefore, that every military authority, without a single exception, whom we have consulted, has reported in favour of evacuation.

But this is not all. Some time ago the Cabinet unanimously came to the conclusion that the war could not be carried on by a body so large as the Cabinet. A War Committee was therefore appointed. The views of the military authorities came before this Committee, two of whose members, the Prime Minister and the First Lord of the Admiralty, were opposed in the strongest possible way to evacuation; yet this Committee reported unanimously in favour of acting upon the advice of our military advisers. Their recommendation was brought before the Cabinet, with the result that on a matter in regard to which delay must be dangerous and may be fatal, no decision has been reached.

I hope that my colleagues will agree with me that the war cannot be carried to a successful issue by methods such as these.

Meanwhile the condition of the forces on the peninsula was aggravated by a blizzard of exceptional severity which raged on November 26th, 27th, 28th and 29th. Two hundred and eighty men were drowned in the trenches at Suvla and many were frozen to death as they stood. Sixteen thousand cases of frost bite and exposure had to be evacuated: 12,000 from Suvla, where the positions were most exposed, and 2,700 and 1,200 from Anzac and Helles respectively. On December 1st Sir Charles Monro telegraphed to Lord Kitchener pressing for a decision and adding:

> There is, however, much to be done, and late season makes time a matter of great urgency. Detailed plans approach completion, but intricate arrangements have still to be made with regard to collection and clearing of shipping, distribution of small craft, embarkation and disposition of troops and material, accommodation on islands, disposal of reinforcements, etc., to say nothing of tactical arrangements.
>
> Experience of recent storms indicates that there is no time to lose. General Birdwood telegraphed yesterday that if evacuation is to be made possible it is essential to take advantage of every fine day from now. If a decision cannot be reached very shortly, it may be equivalent to deciding against evacuation.

It must here be mentioned that on November 25th Sir John de Robeck left the Mediterranean on sick leave, and his command was taken over by Vice-Admiral Wemyss. From November 25th to December 8th Vice-Admiral Wemyss, with remark-able pertinacity [obstinacy], advocated a renewal of the naval attack in a series of telegrams to the First Lord of the Admiralty.

On his return home Sir John de Robeck attended a meeting of the War Council on December 2nd, and his views as to the difficulties of a naval attack were placed before the members of the Council. The decision as to the policy to be pursued was then reserved for the Cabinet which met on the same day. Lord Kitchener, as the result of this Cabinet meeting, telegraphed to Sir Charles Monro:

> Private and secret
> The Cabinet has been considering the Gallipoli situation all today. Owing to the political consequences there is a strong feeling against evacuation, even of a partial character. It is the general opinion that we should retain Cape Helles.
>
> If the Salonica troops are placed at your disposal (up to four divisions) for an offensive operation to improve the position at Suvla, could such operations be carried out in time with a view to making Suvla retainable by obtaining higher positions and greater depth? The Navy will also take the offensive in co-operation.

On December 3rd Sir Charles Monro telegraphed in reply to this proposal as follows:

> I fully recognise the complexity of the situation which has arisen. I do not, however, think that the proposal to employ four fresh divisions in order to gain a more secure position at Suvla can be regarded as an operation offering a reasonable chance of

success. We cannot expect the element of surprise which is so essential to make up for the disadvantages of position under which we labour. The Salonica Divisions could not be ready for active operations on the peninsula until storm weather sets in . . .

In respect of naval co-operation, the character of the terrain on the peninsula is such that naval guns cannot search the Turkish positions. The fire of howitzers would be needed to do so effectively. The many deep ravines and gullies are very favourable for the concealment and protection of the Turkish reserves, and for their rapid transference in case of bombardment. Nor do I think the supply of the Turks on the peninsula by the two lines of supply available to them could be prevented by naval action.

On December 7th the Cabinet decided to evacuate the positions at Suvla and Anzac only and to retain that at Cape Helles. This decision, Lord Curzon told us, was taken mainly on the advice of Lord Kitchener, who had then returned.

The decision of the Cabinet was communicated to Sir Charles Monro on December 7th, and to Vice-Admiral Wemyss on December 8th. The Vice-Admiral, in reply, persisted in recommending that the naval attack should be attempted, and in the course of his telegram to the First Lord of the Admiralty on December 8th stated:

The Navy is prepared to force the Straits and control them for an indefinite period, cutting off all Turkish

supplies which now find their way to the peninsula
either by sea from the Marmora or across the
Dardanelles from Asiatic to European shore. The only
line of communications left would be the road along
the Isthmus of Bulair, which can be controlled almost
entirely from the Sea of Marmora and the Gulf of
Xeros. What is offered the Army, therefore, is the
practical, complete severance of all Turkish lines of
communication, accompanied by the destruction of
the large supply depots on the shore of the
Dardanelles.

In the first instance I strongly advocated that the
naval attack should synchronize with an army
offensive, and if the Army will be prepared to attack
in the event of a favourable opportunity presenting
itself, nothing more need be required of them. The
Navy here is prepared to undertake this operation
with every assurance of success. If the units as
described in your letter of 24th November can be
provided, these hopes of success are greatly increased,
and the possible losses greatly diminished.

The unanimous military opinion referred to has, I
feel certain, been greatly influenced, and naturally so,
by the military appreciations of Sir Charles Monro.
These I have not seen, but their purport I have
gathered in course of conversations. The Corps
Commanders, I know, view the evacuation with the
greatest misgiving. The forcing of the Dardanelles, as
outlined in my telegrams, has never been put before
them, and I am convinced that, after considering the
certain results which would follow a naval success,

they would favour an attack on the lines indicated, especially in view of the undoubted low morale of the Turkish Peninsula army, of which we have ample evidence ...

The very extensive German propaganda being pursued all over the Near East, accompanied by the expenditure of vast sums of money, is not, I feel convinced, being undertaken merely as a side issue to the European war.

A position of stalemate on both fronts of the principal theatres of war appears the natural outcome of the present situation. This opinion is freely expressed in the higher military circles in Greece, and would therefore appear to be fostered by the Germans—a significant point.

By surrendering our position here, when within sight of victory, we are aiding the enemy to obtain markets the possession of which may enable her to outlast the Allies in the war of exhaustion now commencing.

A successful attack would once and for all disperse those clouds of doubt, a large amount of shipping would be released, and the question of Greece and Egypt settled.

I do not know what has been decided about Constantinople, but if the Turks could be told that we were in the Marmora to prevent its occupation by the Germans, such a course would inevitably lead to disruption, and therefore weakness amongst them.

I fear the effect on the Navy would be bad.

Although no word of attack has passed my lips

except to my immediate staff and admirals, I feel sure that every officer and man would feel that the campaign had been abandoned without sufficient use having been made of our greatest force, viz., the Navy.

The position is so critical that there is no time for standing on ceremony, and I suggest that General Birdwood, the officer who would now have to carry out the attack or evacuation which is now ordered, be asked for his appreciation.

The logical conclusion, therefore, is the choice of evacuation or forcing the Straits. I consider the former disastrous tactically and strategically, and the latter feasible, and, so long as troops remain at Anzac, decisive.

I am convinced that the time is ripe for a vigorous offensive, and I am confident of success.

To this strongly worded representation Mr Balfour, then First Lord of the Admiralty, replied on December 10th that, as the Admiralty were not prepared to authorise the Navy, single-handed, attempting to force the Narrows and acting in the Sea of Marmora, cut off from supplies, the decision of the Government to evacuate Suvla and Anzac would not be further questioned by the Admiralty in view of the individual and combined appreciation of the responsible Generals, and the great strain thrown on naval and military resources by the operations in Greece. The retention of Cape Helles and the mouth of the Straits would enable another attack to be started later, working on a different plan, should the Government decide to undertake it. And on the same day the then First Sea Lord, Sir Henry Jackson, telegraphed to Vice-Admiral Wemyss as follows:

> Your telegram has been very carefully considered. I personally agree with your appreciation of German designs in the East, and I view with deepest regret the abandonment of Suvla and Anzac. But the military authorities, including Birdwood, are clear that they cannot be made tenable against an increased artillery fire, while the Admiralty hold that the naval arguments against forcing the Straits are overwhelming. Naval authorities here are convinced that, while success is most doubtful, very heavy losses are certain, and it must be remembered that nothing would have a worse effect on our Eastern position than a serious check to the Government.

The evacuation of Suvla and Anzac was at once proceeded with, men, guns, and stores being gradually withdrawn. The final embarkation was fixed for Saturday and Sunday, December 18th and 19th. On the Sunday a covering attack was made by the forces at Cape Helles, at a cost of 283 casualties. By 5.30 am on Monday, December 20th, the last man had quitted the trenches. That night the weather broke. A heavy gale blew from the south, accompanied by torrents of rain. Water rushed through the trenches at Suvla and Anzac, and the landing stages at Suvla, Anzac, and Cape Helles were washed away by heavy seas.

On December 20th Sir Charles Monro telegraphed to Lord Kitchener urging the evacuation of Cape Helles on the ground that this "would greatly facilitate the reorganisation of the Dardanelles army, would lead immediately to reduced expenditure, and would liberate a large quantity of freight"; and that this army, "when rested and reorganised, would constitute a valuable asset in a central position, ready to strike either in France or wherever demanded by the situation." On December 22nd evacuation was also recommended by the General Staff in a memorandum, in which they pointed out that:

> The arrival of gun ammunition and of fresh guns to help the enemy will, moreover, greatly add to the difficulties in the way of holding on to Helles at all. Not only have munitions arrived from Germany, but artillery which had been previously opposed to Suvla and Anzac will be moved to act against our forces cooped up in the thoroughly bad position they now occupy at the southern end of the peninsula. Wastage, heavy before, will become greater. The troops, furthermore, are perfectly well aware that the Dardanelles undertaking has definitely failed, and, realising that they have no hope of advancing or of causing the enemy any serious injury, will become dispirited. There will be serious risk that the enemy will make a successful attack, and may, under the circumstances, cause us a disaster. The necessity of concentration of effort, if this war

is to be brought to a successful conclusion, has been drawn attention to in recent papers prepared by the General Staff, and there is no object in labouring this point afresh; retention of Helles means dispersion, not concentration of effort. The General Staff therefore recommend that the Gallipoli Peninsula should be entirely evacuated, and with the least possible delay.

We have indicated that the retention of Cape Helles had been advocated mainly on naval grounds. Vice-Admiral Wemyss and Commodore Keyes held a different opinion, which was strengthened after the evacuation of Suvla and Anzac by the consideration of the heavy wastage occurring daily in the VIIIth Army Corps. From December 20th to January 7th the casualties incurred amounted to 345 killed and 1,178 wounded, a total of 1,523, or a daily average of 18 killed and 62 wounded. Vice-Admiral Wemyss therefore advised evacuation unless the Achi Baba position could be captured, and this Sir Charles Monro considered impracticable.

On December 23rd the War Committee decided to evacuate Cape Helles, and their decision was approved by the Cabinet on the 27th. The evacuation was completed on January 8th.

It is not, we think, necessary to give details of the evacuation, these being embodied in Sir Charles Monro's despatch of March 6th, 1916.

In the course of this despatch Sir Charles Monro wrote:

The entire evacuation of the peninsula had now been completed. It demanded for its successful realisation two important military essentials, viz., good luck and skilled, disciplined organisation; and they were both forthcoming to a marked degree at the hour needed. Our luck was in the ascendant by the marvellous spell of calm weather which prevailed. But we were able to turn to the fullest advantage these accidents of fortune.

Lieutenant-General Sir Wm. Birdwood and his Corps Commanders elaborated and prepared the orders in reference to the evacuation with a skill, competence, and courage which could not have been surpassed, and we had a further stroke of good fortune in being associated with Vice-Admiral Sir J. de Robeck, KCB, Vice-Admiral Wemyss, and a body of naval officers whose work remained throughout this anxious period at that standard of accuracy and professional ability which is beyond the power of criticism or cavil [objection].

The line of communication staff, both military and naval, represented respectively by Lieutenant-General E. A. Altham, CB, CMG, Commodore M. S. Fitzmaurice, RN, principal Naval Transport Officer, and Captain H. V. Simpson, RN, Superintending Transport Officer, contributed to the success of the operation by their untiring zeal and conspicuous ability.

The members of the Headquarters Staff showed themselves, without exception, to be officers with whom it was a privilege to be associated; their competence, zeal, and devotion to duty were uniform and unbroken.

In these words of well-deserved commendation of officers and men the name of Sir Charles Monro himself should be included.

ROLE OF THE FRENCH TROOPS

Our narrative of events would be incomplete without a reference to the important part taken by the French troops in the operations on the Gallipoli Peninsula.

On the afternoon of April 24th a regiment of the French division was disembarked at Kum Kale under the guns of the French fleet, and remained ashore till the morning of the the 26th, when it re-embarked. The French captured 500 prisoners, and their landing diverted the fire of the Asiatic guns from Morto Bay and Beach V to Kum Kale, thus contributing to the success of the British landings. On the evening of April 26th the main disembarkation of the French division was begun at Beach V, our Allies occupying the right of the Helles front. Sir Ian Hamilton's despatch, dated May 20th, 1915, describes the landings and subsequent operations up to May 6th. Therein he referred to the loyal and energetic support afforded him by Général d'Amade, who commanded the French force, and added:

> During the fighting which followed the landing of the French division at Sedd-el-Bahr no troops could have acquitted themselves more creditably under very trying circumstances and under very heavy losses than those working under the orders of M. le Général d'Amade.

In May a second French division reinforced the first, Général Gouraud relieving Général d'Amade on May 14th and assuming command of the whole of the French force. One brigade of this second division arrived at Helles on May 8th, and the other on May 12th. On the latter date Sir Ian Hamilton telegraphed to Lord Kitchener that the French casualties from April 25th to date amounted to 246 officers and 12,364 men out of a total strength engaged of 334 officers and 22,116 men.

There was severe fighting at Helles from June 4th to the end of the month, during which the French troops were conspicuous for their dash and gallantry.

In one action on June 21st their losses amounted to 2,500. On June 30th Général Gouraud was wounded, and the command of the French force devolved upon Général Bailloud. In his despatch of August 26th, 1915, Sir Ian Hamilton referred to Général Gouraud in the following terms:

> Général Gouraud brought a great reputation to our help from the battlefields of the Argonne, and in so doing has added to its lustre. A happy mixture of daring in danger and of calm in crisis, full of energy and resource, he has worked hand in glove with his British comrades in arms, and has earned their respect and affection.

On July 12th and 13th the French troops again distinguished themselves in an attack on the enemy's trenches, capturing a machine gun and 200 prisoners. At this time Général Masnou, commanding the First Division, was mortally wounded.

During the operations early in August the French troops do not appear to have been seriously engaged.

In October one French division was transferred from the peninsula to Salonica, the other division being withdrawn soon afterwards.

While we do not think that the conduct of these troops comes within the scope of our enquiry, we feel bound to record their loyal and generous co-opera-tion, their heavy losses, and their conspicuous gallantry.

WATER SUPPLY

The importance of sea-borne water was recognised by the authorities early in March, when it was known there was little or no water for the troops at Mudros, and provision was then made for supplying it, and also for providing distilling apparatus.

(1) The Headquarters Staff were responsible for providing the tanks to be placed on the beaches to receive the water; also for the necessary pumps

and hoses for pumping out the lighters and for providing mules and water receptacles for carrying the water to the troops.

(2) Naval and military officers were appointed in charge of the beaches, responsible for the landing of all stores, including the water.

Sir William Birdwood had from the first realised the importance of water, and in March he sent Brigadier-General de Lotbinière from Egypt to Mudros to investigate the question of supply at that place. General de Lotbinière, who was the Chief Engineer of the Australian and New Zealand Division in Egypt, came to the conclusion, when the idea of the military expedition was contemplated in March, that sea-borne water would be a necessity. He also realised that piers would be required for landing on the peninsula at Anzac, and made arrangements, with the approval of Sir Ian Hamilton, to hire in Egypt four special steel pontoons to form a pier, and these were ballasted with water stowed in petrol tins.

Unfortunately three of these pontoons were lost on the voyage from Alexandria to Mudros. They were placed in the charge of Commander Mitchell, RN, who was attached to the Australian forces, and he arranged to have them towed by the transports carrying the troops. The weather was bad, and the pontoons, which were difficult to tow, broke adrift, and only one arrived at Mudros. This upset the arrangement so far as a landing pier was concerned, but as regards water supply General de Lotbinière, with the assistance of Admiral Wemyss, obtained at Mudros two large wooden lighters and had them filled with fresh water from the ships.

The arrangements for the supply of water during the operations of April 25th for the troops at Helles and Anzac were organised by General Headquarters in concert with the Generals commanding at Helles and Anzac.

At Helles a moderate supply of water was found on landing and subsequently there does not appear to have been any difficulty with the supply.

At Anzac the supply seems to have been barely sufficient. Surgeon-General Howse, VC, the Assistant Director of Medical Services of the 2nd Australian Division, gave evidence that the health of the men was very greatly impaired by the shortage of water. He thought that a great deal of the illness was attributable to the fact that the average ration of water, for many months at least, was not more than half a gallon a day. His evidence that there was a scarcity of water is corroborated by Lieutenant-Colonel Begg, commanding the New Zealand Field Ambulance, but he differs from General Howse as to the effect on the men's health. Sir William Birdwood had a special officer detailed to look after the water, Major Williams, of the Australian forces, as well as General de Lotbinière.

Search on shore was started immediately on landing, and by the evening three wells were found, yielding a small supply. Elaborate arrangements had to be made at Anzac for the supply of sea-borne water, as shore water was scarce. We think it may be stated that the actual operations at Anzac did not fail for want of water; but during the fighting early in August it is stated in Sir Ian Hamilton's despatch of December 11th, 1915, that all ranks were reduced to one pint a day, which is obviously an inadequate allowance for troops operating in a hot climate and difficult country. After the failure to take the heights at Sari Bahr, when Sir Ian Hamilton thought of sending his reserve troops to Sir William Birdwood to make a second attempt, he had to give up the idea on account of the shortage of water.

The water for the use of the troops at the first landing at Helles and Anzac was brought to the beaches by the Royal Navy. When it had been discharged on the beaches, the responsibility for its storage and distribution rested with the military authorities.

For the landing at Suvla detailed orders concerning the arrangements for water were issued by General Headquarters. The following additional information and directions were given to Sir Frederick Stopford, IXth Army Corps:

> Water is plentiful throughout the Anafarta Valley, but pending the disembarkation of water carts, a number of mules with special 8-gallon water bags will be attached to the units of your command.
>
> GOC [General Officer Commanding] IXth Army Corps will arrange for parties to pump water on shore from water lighters. Copy of the Director of Works memo. on this subject is attached.

Two military landing officers and their assistant military landing officers will be placed at your disposal from units other than those under your command.

The strictest economy must be exercised in regard to drinking water. Under arrangements made by GHQ receptacles filled with water will be landed as early as possible from the ships carrying the mule corps, and will be conveyed to the troops as transport becomes available.

Waterproof tanks of 2,300 gallons capacity, lift and force pumps, will be available on the *Prah*—RE Store Ship—in Kephalos Harbour, and will be forwarded by the Deputy Quartermaster General, GHQ, on request of GOC Corps.

In his despatch of December 11th, 1915, Sir Ian Hamilton mentions that the War Office were asked to send with each division of the IXth Corps and with the 53rd and 54th Territorial Divisions water receptacles for pack transport at the rate of half a gallon per man. He also states that 3,700 mules, together with 1,750 water carts, were provided for the August operations at Anzac and Suvla—this in addition to 950 mules already at Anzac. We understand that no water carts were landed at Suvla, the ground being unsuitable for their use. No pack mules with water bags appear in the landing tables, but some mules were in fact sent.

In Sir Frederick Stopford's operation order of August 3rd the water question was dealt with as follows:

It is anticipated that sufficient water for drinking purposes will be found throughout the Anafarta Valley. This will be supplemented by tanks on shore, and water bags, but supply by these methods is limited. The General Officers commanding will issue instructions as regards the picketing [marking] of wells and springs, as may be found, the prevention of waste of water therefrom, and for the examination by Medical Officers before its issue. Too much stress cannot be laid on the importance of warning all ranks to observe the greatest care against waste of ammunition, food, or water.

For the landing at Suvla on the night of August 6th/7th provision was made for 450 tons of sea-borne fresh water to arrive during the early hours of August 7th as follows:

(a)	The steam water tank *Krini* with with a naval water lighter in tow	250 tons
(b)	Four wooden water lighters equipped with small wooden troughs, pumps and hoses provided by the Army and handed over to the Navy for transport to Suvla, 50 to 60 tons each	200 tons
		450 tons

The motor lighters in which the troops landed also had a certain amount of water on board in bulk, supplemented by water in petrol tins, with the idea that the troops should on landing, if necessary, refill their water-bottles.

The troops, before embarking in the destroyers and motor lighters at Imbros on the evening of the 6th, had their water-bottles (1½ pints) filled, and were told to husband [conserve] the water.

Arrangements were made for the troops to have tea from the destroyers before landing.

The failure of the troops to attain their objectives on August 7th, and especially on the 8th, is thought by some witnesses to be due to a large extent to the exhaustion of the troops from want of water, and on the 9th and 10th there was still difficulty in supplying sufficient water.

But the failure to obtain Hill 112, Ismail Oglu Tepe, on the 7th, the most favourable day for a surprise attack, was not primarily due to want of water, but is attributable to other causes, and is dealt with in another portion of the report.

General Hammersley, commanding the 11th Division, stated:

> The first water obtained from the water lighters was about 3 pm on the 8th. The want of water added very much to the exhaustion of the troops. They had nothing but their water-bottles with them. A certain quantity of water was found, but nothing like enough to assuage their thirst, and the troops were badly exhausted.

General Hammersley stated that he realised the great importance of water before the operations began, but did not take any steps to see where water was to be obtained. He knew that water was being sent ashore in lighters, but he was not informed and did not enquire as to the system of distribution of water when landed. He gathered that the men would have to depend on their water-bottles for 24 hours and upon any local supplies he might find.

General Sitwell, commanding 34th Brigade, stated that before he left Imbros on the evening of the 6th he did not know what the arrangements were for providing water. He informed us that he discovered two wells on August 7th and 8th, from which he watered his Brigade, and a considerable number after that date. From these a good supply of water was forthcoming. The position of the wells and springs seemed to him to be accurately marked on the map issued to the troops.

General Sitwell expressed the opinion that if a proper search had been made for water, sufficient would have been found to enable the attack to be pushed forward on the 8th.

General R. P. Maxwell, commanding 33rd Brigade, in his evidence stated:

> The want of water did not interfere with the operations up to the night of the 7th. The water-bottles were not touched before midday on the 7th.

On the 8th, even with a proper supply of water, he does not think his brigade could have done more, because they were so scattered. "My own men wanted water to recuperate, nothing worse than that."

General Haggard, commanding 32nd Brigade, stated:

> I have read Sir Ian Hamilton's despatch about the wonderful arrangements made for water, but nothing was ever communicated to me. The only thing on the subject of water that I remember is that either the Divisional Commander or his Chief Staff Officer told me I must particularly warn the men that they must husband the water in their water-bottles, because they probably would not get any for 48 hours.

He further stated there was no shortage up to the time he was wounded, which appears to have been in the forenoon [late morning] of the 7th. He did not know whose duty it was to see that water was supplied.

Sir Bryan Mahon, commanding 10th Division, stated that the men had their water-bottles full when they started. On the morning of the 7th they tried without success to get a further supply. Some was given to them by a destroyer which came inshore on the afternoon of that day. On the morning of the 8th they obtained a further quantity. A good well was discovered on the 8th about halfway down to the sea, but there was a difficulty in distributing it owing to the want of mules. The troops could not have operated on the 8th, but after that they could have gone on so far as water was concerned.

General Hill, commanding 31st Brigade, stated that his men got no water except what they had had in their water-bottles from the time that they landed at about 8 am on the 7th until 3 pm on the 8th, and they suffered very badly, and they could not advance on the 8th owing to that. The Dublin Fusiliers brought them up some water, about half a bottle per man. They found two wells, but the Turks were sniping most of the time. They had to get water under fire, and could not organise any good system of getting it. It was impossible to do more on the 8th, but they could have done more on the 7th. The men went out at night to the two wells and got a certain amount of water, enough to enable them to do some cooking, but it was not a big supply. If they had pushed on on the 7th they might very likely have reduced the sniping.

We think that want of water was not the sole cause of the failure of the troops to advance further on the 7th; but on the 8th, with the exception of the 34th Brigade, the troops had been so long without water that they could hardly have been expected to undertake any serious operation. There is some reason to suppose that if the objectives had been gained on the 7th more water would have been obtainable from wells and springs, and the sniping of the known wells would have been much reduced, if not stopped altogether.

The failure of the supply of sea-borne water for the troops is attributed by Sir Frederick Stopford and other military officers to the fact that only two of the five water lighters arrived on August 7th, that they grounded on a sandbank at 80–100 yards from the shore, and that as the hoses provided were not long enough to reach the beach, no water was available for use from them until the morning of the 8th. Colonel Western, the Principal Military Landing Officer, at 5.30 pm on August 7th, sent the following telegram to Sir Frederick Stopford:

> Water for troops essential to success of undertaking. None has been landed. Can you arrange with the Admiral that this be landed at Beach A? GHQ directs 1,000 water bags containing 8 gallons each be sent to Anzac. Suggest half be sent here and ship's balance be sent to Anzac. Casualty clearing station now at Beach C. I would add nothing has yet been landed except small arm ammunition.

In a statement by Admiral Keyes, Commander Ashby, Naval Transport Officer, informed us that the last water lighter left Kephalos at 4 am on the 7th, and should have arrived by 7 am. Further, Admiral Keyes stated:

> I cannot exactly say when the lighters reached the beaches, and I can produce no evidence to show that they were beached before the afternoon of the 7th. I can state quite definitely from my own observation that water lighters were delivering water to the shore at three different places on the afternoon of the 7th—namely, at one of the northern beaches (probably A west), under Mount Falcon (Lala Baba)

in the south-east corner of Suvla Bay, and at C Beach, south of Nebrunesi Point.

This evidence is confirmed by statements by Captain Lambart, RN, and other naval officers. No doubt one lighter stranded on a rocky ledge under Lala Baba, as Admiral Keyes stated:

> The water lighter was some little distance from the shore, which its hose would not reach. I boarded it and used the picket [patrol] boat I was in to tow it into a position from which its hose would reach the shore. I remarked that the water was being wasted, as water bottles were being filled direct from the hose, and there was no proper control over the shore end of the hose.

Probably this stranded lighter may account for part of the evidence on this subject given by military witnesses, but we think the evidence of the naval officers is correct, and that on the afternoon of the 7th water was being discharged from three lighters to the beaches. This is confirmed by Colonel Western, Principal Military Landing Officer, who stated: "I think the supply was fairly tight, but it was getting the water from the beach to the troops where the block occurred. There were not sufficient receptacles."

From the evidence of Major White, commanding the 68th Field Company Royal Engineers, which was detailed to receive the water lighters, it appears possible that some of the lighters discharging water on August 7th were supplied by the Navy.

The original project as described by Sir Frederick Stopford was to use water carts as receptacles on the beach, but as none of these were landed this could not be done. Wooden tanks were provided by General de Lotbinière in each of the four water lighters. They were too small and leaked badly; eventually, naval carpenters made them water-tight, and the Navy supplied tanks and baths. In one instance the Commander of a Destroyer, *The Foxhound*, ordered one of his tanks to be cut out and taken ashore and it was used for the storage of water.

The evidence shows there was a great deal of confusion on the beaches. The men not being able to get water quickly enough, owing to the absence of receptacles, took out their knives and pricked holes in the hoses. Colonel Western considers there was a serious want of discipline, and a lack of power of command on the part of the regimental commanders and officers, and this is confirmed by naval officers, especially by Captain Carver, RN, who acted for a time as beach-master.

Major-General Poett, as Deputy Adjutant and Quartermaster-General, had the general responsibility for provision of water to the troops, but he states that with regard to sea-borne water he had no responsibility until it reached the beaches, because General Headquarters were, with the Navy, responsible for landing water and mules. He should have ascertained when the water was likely to be landed, and made arrangements for its reception and distribution. Sir Frederick Stopford states that General

Poett did not write any appreciation in detail as to how the water was to be distributed and that he did not discuss the question verbally with General Poett. He [Stopford] said:

> I find it difficult to say exactly what was in my mind, knowing what has happened since, but my impression is that the water there did not cause me any anxiety because I was informed there was plenty of water. I was informed there were four lighters and mules coming, and I rather thought the mules would be wanted for getting it up country. When I found that water had failed, and had not been landed, to my great astonishment, I sent for General Poett and asked: 'How do we stand with regard to food?' He said: 'We have one day to go on with,' and I said: 'Very well, we must stop everything else for water.' My anxiety till then was more in connection with food, because I did not anticipate there would be any difficulty about water.

With regard to the distribution of water he said: "I did not go into it personally; perhaps I ought to have done." Water carts were brought by the ships which carried the mules, but they were not landed and Sir Frederick Stopford, in his evidence, stated that they could not have been used by reason of the nature of the country.

The arrangements made by General Headquarters for landing mules with water bags for the supply of troops in the first instance were impeded by the delay in landing the 10th Division and by the necessity of sending mules to Anzac owing to the urgent signal received from General Headquarters on the afternoon of August 7th. Sir Frederick Stopford and Admiral Christian think that this was the chief cause for the want of mules on that day.

According to Admiral Christian's evidence, only one ship with pack mules and 8-gallon water bags on board—the *Dundrennan*—arrived at Suvla Bay on August 7th. Admiral Keyes gives as the reason for this that big ships had to be berthed near the net to avoid the risk of being torpedoed. Consequently, as the protected area was limited, it was arranged not to have at Suvla more ships than could be unloaded at the time.

The result was that sufficient mules were not landed, but Captain Unwin, RN, VC, who was in charge, states that they commenced to land mules at about 10 am on the 7th at A (New Beach), and they were hard at it the whole time; he was not able to give an estimate of the total number of mules landed on the 7th, but Sir Frederick Stopford says that 500 were landed. No effort, apparently, was made to organise fatigue parties to supplement the paucity of mules.

Water in bulk and in petrol tins was provided in the motor lighters, but we have been unable to ascertain whether orders were issued by the battalion and company officers to the men to refill their water-bottles before landing. In some cases the naval officers in the lighters warned the NCOs to have the water-bottles filled, but apparently nothing was done. There is no evidence, however, that the water-bottles were not full when the men landed.

Sir Frederick Stopford said that the lighters were ordered away at once before the water could be used for refilling the bottles. He said:

> The water, I think, in those lighters was not intended to be used on shore, but was intended for the troops while they were on board. It was never intended for a shore supply, that is my impression, or I never heard of it.

The steps to be taken to explore the local resources for water were entrusted to the Chief Engineer of the Corps. General Painter informed us in a telegram that he detailed parties to search and dig for water in the neighbourhood of the beaches, but we have no evidence as to what was done on August 7th by these parties.

Sir Beauvoir de Lisle, who relieved Sir Frederick Stopford on the 15th, stated that there he experienced no trouble about water.

> There were wells within a quarter of a mile of the shore, which I had opened out. On the hill Keritch Tepe Sirt, there were two wells 400 feet higher than the sea. But on this side, between Keritch Tepe Sirt and the Salt Lake, there were as many wells as you liked to dig. You had not to go more than 15 feet before you got as much water as you wanted. Inside the area which they occupied on the first day they had only to scratch the sand to get as much water as they wanted. On the shore, within 100 yards of high-water mark, you had only to dig

the sand 4 feet down to get water. All that means bad staff work, because the Royal Engineers could have found that out as easily as I could. At one place, if they had only taken a mess tin and scraped it with their hands they would have come to water. The difficulties about water were very much exaggerated.

This is confirmed also by General Sitwell, who found sufficient water for his brigade (the 34th).

The discovery of water was, however, a gradual process, and we doubt whether on August 7th and 8th sufficient water could have been found from local resources alone to make good the deficiency of the sea-borne supply. The failure to supply sea-borne water to the troops is attributable to the fact that:

(1) The landing of the mules which were to supply the troops with water was much delayed.
(2) No arrangements had been made for the distribution of water in case of the failure of the mules to land in time.
(3) Suitable receptacles had not been provided on the beaches to receive the water from the lighters.
(4) No fatigue parties were organised to distribute such water as might be available in case of scarcity of mules.

We think that the Corps Commander and his Administrative Staff did not sufficiently realise the absolute importance of water, until Colonel Western sent a telegram to Sir Frederick Stopford at 5.15 pm on the 7th to say troops were short of water. This is corroborated by General Poett, who stated:

> When I left Sir Frederick Stopford at about 11 o'clock on the morning of the 7th he was not anxious about water, because he had been told definitely that water was plentiful, but he was most anxious that I should get the munitions on shore.

Possibly they may have been misled by information they had from the Headquarters Staff. General Stopford said:

> As regards the supply of water which came, till it was landed, I had nothing to do with it, and I assumed that the necessary arrangements had been made by the Commander-in-Chief, who was responsible for the plans.

He explained that when at Imbros he had made enquiries about the water, and found the Headquarters Staff were responsible for the water coming to Imbros and the Navy was responsible for getting it ashore.

> The General Officer who made the plan of the campaign was responsible for telling the Navy when and where the water was required. If I had been told it was a matter of duty to know what water I required, and get the mules and lighters, I should have done so, but I understood it was to be done by the Headquarters Staff.

He said that two lighters left Imbros with the troops
and that he did not know whether Admiral Christian
had any orders as to when he was to land the water,
and did not talk it over with him. In another answer
he said:

> According to my recollection the sole instructions I
> received about the water supply were in the secret
> instructions, 22nd July, that water was plentiful
> throughout the Anafarta Valley. I was never informed
> that water would be scarce, and the responsibility,
> according to the paper and instructions you get for
> such a supply of water as came from the sea, rested
> with the General Headquarters Staff.

General Poett stated:

> The orders for the landing of the personnel, the
> ammunition, the supplies, and the arrangement for
> providing sea-borne water were made by the General
> Headquarters Staff, presumably after consultation
> with the Admiral, and with his full approval. These
> orders were in great detail, and appear to cover the
> ground, assuming them to be carried out. Not only
> did General Headquarters assume all responsibility for
> the landing orders, but they appointed a special staff
> to assist in carrying them out. I am inclined to think
> the inaccurate information in General Headquarters'
> Orders that water was plentiful misled everybody. It
> must not be lost sight of that the food and
> ammunition had also to be considered. To the best of

my recollection I received the detailed Orders, I
think, on the 5th, but I will not be sure. We got them
some days before the landing.

General Poett understood that the Navy was responsible for bringing the water to the beaches, but he did
not take any steps before the landing to get into communication with the naval authorities in order to
ascertain exactly what was going to be done. He took
it for granted that as the orders were drafted by
General Headquarters in concert with the Navy, and
as they had their own Principal Military Landing
Officer and Beach Master, all details would be arranged
between those two officers. He considered that his
responsibility would begin with the distribution of
the water.

We think that Sir Frederick Stopford and his staff
failed to realise the importance of having sea-borne
water ready for issue to the troops early on the 7th,
they may have been misled by General Headquarters
saying that water was plentiful in the Anafarta Valley,
but it was evident that until the valley was captured
water would not be obtainable there.

The supply of sea-borne water was, however,
specifically undertaken by General Headquarters in
concert with the Navy, and it rested with them to
place the lighters in positions from which water could
be delivered on to the beaches and to land the pack
mules and filled water bags as required by the Officer
Commanding the IXth Corps.

FOOD

The circumstances in which the supply had to be made are described by Sir John Cowans, the Quartermaster-General to the Forces, as abnormal and peculiar. The details of the arrangements for the supply of stores, the amount shipped and the scale of daily rations are set out in the statement of Lieutenant-Colonel H. F. P. Percival, Assistant Director of Supplies. A large proportion of the meat supplied was preserved or tinned, and the precautions taken to secure that it was of good quality are described by Brigadier-General Long, then Director of Supplies and Transport.

These provided for an inspection of the meat before being shipped, and in order to secure a proper examination by competent persons it was arranged, with the consent of the Local Government Board, that it should be made by or with the assistance of the local authorities and their medical staff.

In the case of purchases from South America, the Local Government Board sent out some of their inspectors, who were at the factories during the whole of the time at the War Office expense, supervising the packing of meat and satisfying themselves as to its quality.

The only serious complaints which were brought to our notice are with regard to the absence of canteens, the deficient supply of condiments, and the quality of a certain brand of South American tinned meat.

When the hot weather began in Gallipoli there was a great deal of sickness, chiefly of the type of diarrhoea or dysentery, and a continued diet of tinned meat, even if of good quality, became distasteful. If it were salt and stringy, as was the case with some of the meat, it was still more distasteful, and, if eaten, made the men more liable to these diseases. As will be seen by the scale of rations set out in Lieutenant-Colonel Percival's statement, provision was made for the variation of the ration by giving equivalents, and these equivalents were provided. But this could only be done within limits, and a wider variation of the diet could only be attained by the establishment of canteens. If canteens had been established and this variation obtained at an earlier date, there would have been a reduction of the sickness.

The first request for canteens was made on May 27th, and it was suggested that they should be provided by the Canteen and Mess Co-operative Society.

It was proposed to finance them by using some money of the South African Garrison Institute Fund. Any money used would only be a loan, as it would be recouped from the sum paid by the men for supplies. It was alleged in evidence before us that obstacles were put in the way of supplying canteens by Sir Charles Harris, the Assistant Financial Secretary at the War Office, but we find there was no foundation for such statement.

At first Lord Kitchener was disinclined to send canteens, but after pressure from Sir John Cowans he consented to the use of £10,000. The Treasury later on advanced £50,000 for the same purpose. In the result ten ships carrying canteen stores to the value of about £90,000 went out to the peninsula between the 16th July and the 4th November, 1915. Sir John Cowans also told us that the troops were not getting the ordinary but a varied ration. He said: "It was a very good ration, and we had in addition fresh vegetables from Bulgaria and Greece and Egypt." There was also a complaint that more condiments and sauces were not supplied for the use of the Australian and New Zealand troops. Colonel Percival gave evidence that these articles would have been supplied if asked for by the Deputy Quartermaster-General of the force. They were not asked for, and we have no evidence that any request for them was ever conveyed to him.

The only complaint of the quality of food that we have had before us is in respect of a certain brand of South American tinned meat spoken of as "Fray Bentos". Two other brands of tinned meat were mentioned as not satisfactory, but there was not sufficient evidence about them to enable us to come to a conclusion.

The "Fray Bentos" meat is described by Sir Alexander Godley in the following terms:

> It was very, very salt, and very stringy bully. I think it
> was of inferior quality. I have eaten very much worse
> bully beef than that in previous campaigns. I have
> been campaigning and I have eaten much worse beef.
> Still it was not good, and certainly the men did not
> like it.

This agrees with all the other evidence in describing the meat as salt and stringy. When the weather was hot and the men inclined to suffer from diarrhoea and dysentery such meat was very distasteful, and they would not eat it. Many of them, while in hospital in England, stated that they could trace an increase of illness on the days when this brand and the other two mentioned were served out, and a decrease when they got other meat. No evidence except this was given as to the quality of the other two brands.

Lieutenant-Colonel Myers, the Assistant Director of Medical Services to the New Zealand forces, who took these statements from the men, was of the opinion that they would be able to trace such increase and diminution. Sir Alexander Godley, speaking not, of course, as a medical witness, said that he did not notice any difference in the health of the men if they had Fray Bentos one day and fresh meat the next; and Captain Ritchie, a medical officer with the New Zealand force, on being asked if he had noticed the change, said:

> The only marked change that I saw in that way was at Headquarters. Everyone of us had diarrhoea very bad the day after we were given fresh meat for the first time.

When asked if he had noticed anything of the ill-effects to the men's health from the Fray Bentos, he said: "No, it may not have been due to the meat that the men had diarrhoea, it may have been the combination of the meat, the method of living, and water; but the meat was not nice, it was a bit salt." He was serving as a sanitary officer and did not attend to the medical treatment of the men. Fray Bentos is a well-known brand, and we have ascertained from Colonel Percival that it has been issued to all troops in all theatres of war (including France) since the beginning of the War.

We think the result of this to be that there was nothing actively injurious to health in the meat; but it was of poor quality, and from being salt and stringy it caused some intestinal irritation, and so contributed to diarrhoea.

It must be remembered that the Australian and New Zealand troops had been some months at Anzac when the hot weather began, continually in the trenches, and without proper opportunities of rest, and that their energy and activity had been overtaxed. They were, therefore, probably very liable to ill-effects from food unsuitable to such weather.

We have no evidence that any complaint was made by the responsible military or medical authorities in Gallipoli while the meat was being issued, but a complaint was made to the Quartermaster-General's department in November, 1915, by the High Commissioner for New Zealand, and samples of that brand of meat were examined by experts, including the Principal Medical Officer of the inspection department of the Local Government Board, and found satisfactory.

In December, 1915, the complaint was renewed from the office of the High Commissioner for New Zealand, and it was stated that when preserved meat from New Zealand or Australia was supplied the health of the men improved. The Quartermaster-General's department agreed to consider offers of New Zealand meat, and also proposed a conference between representatives of the New Zealand Government, the Food Inspection Department of the Local Government Board, and representatives of the War Office to examine all brands of meat and discuss the whole question. In reply the War Office were informed by the High Commissioner for New Zealand that the only form of conference which could serve any useful purpose would be one at which actual samples of the meat buried by the troops or thrown overboard from the transports could be examined. It was, of course, impossible to get these samples, and so no conference was held.

After the examination in November, 1915, an alteration was made in the specification of the meat and the percentage of salt reduced.

These were the only complaints received about this meat, and since the alteration in the specification no complaints have been received by the Quartermaster-General's department.

MEDICAL ARRANGEMENTS

The medical arrangements for the Dardanelles Expedition were at first under the control of Surgeon-General Birrell, who was selected for the position by Sir Alfred Keogh, the Director-General of the Army Medical Service. Sir Alfred Keogh described the course adopted in such appointments as follows. When it became necessary to appoint a Director of Medical Services for a foreign expedition he examined the list of officers eligible for the position, and from his knowledge of their qualifications selected the one whom he considered most fitted for the position. This was the course adopted in the case of Surgeon-General Birrell, who had considerable experience of active service.

He was appointed Director of Medical Services on the 15th March, 1915, and arrived at Alexandria on April 1st, 1915. The Commander-in-Chief and the General Staff left in two or three days for Mudros, but the Director of Medical Services together with the rest of the Administrative Staff who were then at Alexandria were left behind. Lieutenant-Colonel Keble, one of Surgeon-General Birrell's subordinates, went with the General Staff to Mudros. There were matters connected with the provision of hospital accommodation in Egypt which had to be settled between Surgeon-General Birrell and Surgeon-General Ford, the Director of Medical Services in Egypt, under whose control they were to be.

On the whole we think it would have been better if Surgeon-General Birrell had gone to Mudros with the General Staff and left a subordinate to deal with hospital questions in Alexandria; but Colonel Keble, who went to Mudros, and from whose notes the scheme for dealing with the casualties was drafted, is spoken of by Sir Ian Hamilton as a very competent officer.

Before the Deputy Adjutant-General and Director of Medical Services arrived at Mudros, a scheme prepared by one of the officers of the General Staff, based upon an estimate of 3,000 casualties, was shown to Lieutenant-Colonel Keble, who declined to consider it, as he thought that it was the duty of the Director of Medical Services and his Staff to prepare such a scheme and not that of the General Staff. He prepared notes of a scheme of evacuation based upon an estimate of 10,000 casualties. He had not been able before the arrival of the Administrative Staff to submit these notes to the Chief of the General Staff; and he handed them to the Deputy Adjutant-General and Director of Medical Services as soon as they arrived. There is some conflict of evidence as to whether the estimate of 10,000 was made in the first instance by the General Staff or by Lieutenant-Colonel Keble. We do not think that this is material, as the estimate was accepted by both the General and the Administrative Staffs, and Surgeon-General Birrell was so informed by an officer of the General Staff.

The Director of Medical Services arrived on April 18th, and Colonel Keble's notes were examined by him and the Deputy Adjutant-General. From these notes a draft scheme was made out and passed by the Chief of the General Staff on April 19th. This document is as follows:

> The medical arrangements in connection with the landing of the British Force are at present as follows:

> 1. With each covering force the bearer sub-division of a field ambulance and one tent sub-division, with as much medical and surgical material as can be man-handled by the personnel; giving a total of 150 medical personnel with each covering force.

2. At 2 pm on the day of landing the personnel of the casualty clearing station (one for the 29th Division, one for the Australian and New Zealand Army Corps) will be landed with as much medical and surgical material as can be manhandled.

3. When the remainder of the division lands, the rest of the field ambulance and the equipment of the casualty clearing station will be put on shore as soon as it can be disembarked.

4. Two hospital ships will be available:
   With the 29th Division, *Sicilia*: accommodation, 400 serious cases.
   With the Australian and New Zealand Army Corps, *Gascon*: accommodation, 300 serious cases. The latter ship is expected here on Tuesday.

5. I understand from the Senior Naval Transport Officer that the Navy will commence the transport of wounded from the shore to the ships at about 2 pm. The means of evacuation are as follows:
   Three launches, each capable of holding 12 cots, are available for the 29th Division, and the same number for the Australian and New Zealand Army Corps. These launches are to be towed to the hospital ships and other ships in which the men are to be accommodated.

6. This provision for the evacuation of casualties from the Force appears to be altogether inadequate, and I would strongly urge that the following proposals should be sanctioned:
   (i) B2 *Caledonia*   470 serious cases
        B7 *Aragon*   200 serious cases
        B9 *Dongola*   200 serious cases

should be allotted to the 29th Division for the accommodation of their wounded.

I recommend:

(ii)	That the A25 *Lutzow*	200 serious cases
	A1 *Ionian*	100 serious cases
	some other ship (*Southland?*)	420 serious cases

be allotted to the Australian and New Zealand Army Corps.

(iii) That two more tows of three launches each— equals 72 additional cots—should be provided for the 29th Division and a similar number for the Australian and New Zealand Army Corps.

7. It has previously been proposed to provide the personnel and medical and surgical equipment for the above transports of the 29th Division from Nos 15 and 16 Stationary Hospitals, and the personnel for the transports of the Australian and New Zealand Army Corps from No. 2 Australian Stationary Hospital. These Stationary Hospitals have been wired for.

19th April, 1915   E. M. WOODWARD
                                   Deputy Adjutant-General

This scheme, which was signed by General Woodward, mentions only one hospital ship, the *Sicilia*, for Helles, and one, the *Gascon*, for Anzac; and it will be observed that the number of serious cases for which accommodation was provided amounted to 2,290. No mention is made of the provision for slight cases. Surgeon-General Birrell, in a report to Sir Alfred Keogh, dated April 22nd, gives a fuller account of the arrangements.

REPORT ON MEDICAL ARRANGEMENTS IMPENDING
OPERATIONS, GALLIPOLI PENINSULA

Hospital ships

(*a*) With Naval Division which at the outset is not
undertaking serious operations is the *Somali*.

(*b*) With the Australian and New Zealand Army Corps
is the HS *Gascon*.

(*c*) With the 29th Division is the HS *Sicilia*.

This does not provide accommodation for anything
like the expected casualties, and as for many days it
may be impossible to open stationary hospitals
ashore, I have, for the 29th Division, caused to be
taken over, after evacuation by the fighting troops, the
transports *Caledonia*, *Aragon* and *Dongola*, and have
staffed them from the personnel of the 15th
Stationary Hospital. The medical and surgical
equipment has been divided equally between these
three ships additional to the normal equipment
carried. For the Australian and New Zealand Army
Corps I have caused the *Lutzow*, *Ionian*, *Clan
McGillivray*, and *Seang-Chung* to be taken over. They
will be staffed by the personnel of the 2nd Australian
Stationary Hospital when it arrives. It sailed from
Alexandria on board the *Hindu* on the 20th April.

All these ships can make Alexandria in 48 hours
and Malta in four days.

They can accommodate together with the regular
hospital ships 1,995 serious cases, and at a pinch an

additional 414 cases, or in all 2,409 cases, and 7,300 slightly wounded cases, or a grand total of 9,709 wounded.

If more transports are needed they are available and can be staffed by the 16th Stationary Hospital which sailed on 20th April on *Hindu*, and which is being held in reserve.

The hospital ship *Guildford Castle* has been wired for at Alexandria, and she sailed on 21st April; on arrival she will be used to evacuate the No. 1 Australian Stationary Hospital which is opened at Lemnos, and which is filled to overflowing.

Medical stores

No. 4 advanced depot of medical stores goes with the Australian and New Zealand Corps on the *Hymettus*, which, however, is ashore and may not be got off.

No. 5 advanced depot of medical stores sailed from Alexandria on 20th April on *Hindu*, and is for the supply of the 29th Division.

Evacuation

Evacuation of casualties will be direct to Egypt and Malta.

Casualty Clearing Stations

No. 11 Casualty Clearing Station goes ashore with the 29th Division, and operates near the beach, as does the Australian CCS with the Australian and New Zealand Army Corps.

Future proposals
After the initial operations the three hospital ships, *Sicilia, Gascon, Guildford Castle* and one other which is asked for, will act as ferry boats for sick and wounded between the three stationary hospitals which will be established according to regiments on the Gallipoli Peninsula and the bases at Alexandria and Malta. It is impossible to move the No. 1 Australian Stationary Hospital at Lemnos owing to the number of infectious cases therein, viz., small pox, 2; scarlet fever, 3; diphtheria, 1; measles, 14; mumps, 2.

Evacuation as affected by military operations
During the landing and the actions immediately subsequent thereto, the wounded may have to suffer hardships as it will be impossible to evacuate from shore to ships till the fighting troops have been landed, and even when they have been got aboard it may not be expedient to send the ships away to the bases till our foothold is secure, as during the first two or more days no wheeled transport can go ashore. The strain on the whole medical personnel will be exceedingly great.

Requirements

1. I think the supply of dressings will not prove to be adequate if fighting is sustained, and therefore recommend that 100 boxes of reserve dressings be sent out.
2. As the water on the Gallipoli Peninsula is not above suspicion filter water carts should be provided for the

stationary hospitals at the rate of two per hospital. Eight will be required.

3.   One more hospital ship will be required to maintain the ferry service.

4.   To provide for casualties and to meet unexpected requirements, at least six medical officers should be sent here for attachment to the stationary hospitals.

Lemnos, *April 22nd*, 1915   W. G. BIRRELL,

Surgeon-General

This report mentions a larger number of hospital ships as available in the first two or three days and states the accommodation provided in all the ships mentioned to be: serious cases, 2,409; slight cases, 7,300; making a total of 9,709.

AVAILABILITY AND STAFFING OF HOSPITAL SHIPS

According to Surgeon-General Birrell's evidence the *Somali* and the *Sudan* were available at or immediately after the landing; while the *Guildford Castle* arrived on April 26th and the *Delta* on April 27th, making six hospital ships in all. In addition to these hospital ships, there were seven transports which were allotted, four to Anzac and three to Helles. If any further accommodation were required for the wounded, it had to be obtained by using other transports which had brought the troops to the peninsula.

This report states that the transports mentioned therein were taken up because it might be impossible to open stationary hospitals ashore for many days, and specifies the accommodation on the transports for serious cases. Both Surgeon-General Birrell and Lieutenant-Colonel Keble, however, gave evidence that, although there was accommodation for the estimated number of serious cases, the transports were not provided with the appliances necessary for the treatment of such cases, and also that such appliances could not be obtained at the time. It seems clear that, although this accommodation was provided, it was not expected that it would be required, as the medical staff shared the anticipation of all the military authorities that, if the landing were successfully effected, a rapid advance would be made and hospitals would soon be established on land.

In the actual circumstances of the landing the supply of hospital ships was insufficient, and if a landing in force on the peninsula had been contemplated when the expedition left England we think it would have been the duty of the Director of Medical Services to have arranged for a more ample supply. It has, however, been already pointed out that the instructions given to Sir Ian Hamilton by the Secretary of State for War did not contemplate such a landing, and the Director of Medical Services had no information before leaving England upon which he could base his requirements. In his evidence he stated that, if he had received earlier information that heavier casualties were expected, he could have made better preparation. We think that, if the Administrative Staff had accompanied General Headquarters to

Mudros, the Director of Medical Services would have been in a better position to inform himself of the probable operations and to estimate the consequent requirements.

The Director of Medical Services, however, did make arrangements in Egypt for the provision of hospital accommodation for a large number of casualties, and we think that with a little more forethought he might have arranged for the supply of some of the equipment which was afterwards found to be wanting on the transports.

According to Lieutenant-Colonel Keble's evidence, each of the transports which were sent to Helles for the evacuation of the wounded was provided with at least four medical officers. Those which were sent to Anzac were not so provided on their leaving Mudros because the medical personnel intended for them was not available at the time. This personnel came to Mudros on a ship called the *Hindu*, which was unfortunately delayed. When she arrived a request was sent for a boat to transfer the medical staff to the transports, but one could not be obtained, and the transports left without the intended provision of medical officers. Colonel Keble said, however, that there was no reason why the number should not have been made up at Anzac, as the *Hindu* followed them there; and there were also medical officers of the units which could not be landed available for service on the transports.

TRANSPORT ARRANGEMENTS FOR THE SICK AND WOUNDED

At the time of the landing the bearer divisions and the field ambulances landed with the troops, and later the casualty clearing stations and a part of the tent divisions of the field ambulance. With the covering division one tent sub-division landed with the bearer divisions. The intention was that the stationary hospitals should be landed as soon as possible, and that from the first the cases should be sorted, the serious ones going to the hospital ships and the slighter ones to the seven allotted transports and the other transports which it was found necessary to employ.

Three classes of ships were employed for transporting the wounded to the main bases, Alexandria, Malta and England, namely:

Hospital ships

Hospital carriers

Transports, generally called "black ships"

In addition, sweepers and other craft were used to convey the wounded from the beaches to the ships.

The hospital ships were well equipped and gave every satisfaction, and took about five weeks to fit out.

The hospital carriers were hastily improvised; they were used because there was not time to fit them properly as hospital ships. Undoubtedly they were not adapted for the conveyance of serious cases for long distances, but they were fairly satisfactory for short distances. None of these vessels was available at the first landing.

The transports (black ships) which were only intended for the conveyance of light cases, were not properly equipped for serious cases. Many of them were used immediately after the troops had disembarked, and in some cases the horses were left on board. As a rule there were four medical officers on board, with some attendants and stores, but they had no arrangements for dealing with serious cases and were not meant to carry them. Unfortunately, owing to the difficulty of sorting the light from the serious cases, many of the latter were put on board these ships, and this entailed a great deal of suffering.

On the first days of the landing, April 25th, 26th and 27th, the Administrative Staff were again separated from the General Staff. The Commander-in-Chief and the greater part of the General Staff were on board the *Queen Elizabeth*, and the Administrative Staff, including the Director of Medical Services, were left on board the *Arcadian*. According to the evidence this was done because there was not room for the whole staff on board the *Queen Elizabeth*, but the result was that the Director of Medical Services, who was on the *Arcadian*, and was not allowed to use her wireless installation, was unable to give any directions as to the operations for evacuating the wounded. These directions were in consequence given by the General Staff. We think that this was unfortunate and should have been avoided, but we do not attach much importance to the incident, as Surgeon-General Birrell and Colonel Keble say that the General Staff were carrying out

Surgeon-General Birrell's scheme, and that the fact of its being carried out by them, and not by himself, did not substantially interfere with the evacuation and the comfort of the wounded, or prejudicially affect the situation.

Difficulties of sorting the wounded

Hardly any advance was made after the landing, and it was found impossible to carry out the evacuation as intended. It therefore became necessary that all casualties should be evacuated by sea as soon as possible. The casualties began at the very outset of the landing, and many of them occurred in the boats before the men had disembarked. It was impossible to sort the cases as had been intended, and they could not be left on the beaches, which were under shell fire. The selection of serious cases for the hospital ships and lighter cases for the transports could not be carried out. The hospital ships received many slight cases, and what was more serious, many severe cases had, in consequence, to be taken to the transports.

According to General Woodward and Surgeon-General Birrell there were at one time 300 slight cases on the *Gascon*, a hospital ship intended for serious cases, and this probably occurred in other instances. The result was that much suffering was occasioned to the severely wounded men, who were carried on the partially fitted transports. These ships were not fitted or staffed for such cases, and there were no appliances for the surgical treatment or attendance required. Additional hardship

sometimes was occasioned by reason of delay in transferring wounded men from the small craft which took
them from the beach into a transport. Surgeon-
General Howse said that he was informed that in one
case the wounded were taken to four or five transports
before one was found which could receive them, and
a similar instance was mentioned by Admiral Keyes on
the report of Admiral Phillimore.

Numbers of casualties

There is a conflict of evidence as to whether the
number of casualties was greater than was expected.
Sir Ian Hamilton and General Braithwaite say they
were much greater, although the latter gave evidence
that the General Staff estimated them at 10,000. Sir
John Maxwell, speaking of course from hearsay,
expresses the same opinion, and there is other evidence to the same effect. On the other hand,
Surgeon-General Birrell says that in the first few days
the casualties were not more than he had expected,
and the estimate contained in his report to Sir Alfred
Keogh bears out this statement. It may be that it was
not the number of the casualties alone which was
important, but that the number combined with the
necessity of transporting them by sea, and the impossibility of sorting them into slight and serious cases,
caused an unexpected confusion and crowding of the
hospital ships and transports.

The conditions stated above prevailed at both
Helles and Anzac during the early days following the

landing. Throughout the months of May, June and July the evacuation of casualties continued, though, except in the attacks of May 5th and 6th, and June 4th and 28th, the number evacuated was much fewer, and the use of the transports much less. According to the evidence, matters began to improve after the first ten days.

There is no doubt that great difficulties were experienced in the first few days of the operations, and that the wounded suffered in consequence. To what extent this was due to bad arrangements and to what extent it was unavoidable is a difficult question to determine, the evidence being contradictory and too voluminous to be set out in full.

Inadequate medical care

The real substance of the complaints, in our opinion, is the want of medical and nursing attendance and equipment upon the transports. There is evidence as to the want of boats and barges in which to take the wounded from the beach and of tugs or pinnaces [rowing boats] to tow these craft when loaded to the hospital ships and transports, and also as to a want of organisation in ordering them to different hospital ships; but the real complaint seems to us to be the broad fact that men wounded on the peninsula were often many hours or days before their wounds were re-dressed, and did not receive proper medical attention in the meantime.

We think that, during the first few days after the landing in April, difficulty and confusion in collecting the wounded and removing them from the beaches were unavoidable, owing to the failure to push inland and the fact that the beaches and the small craft approaching or leaving the shore were under the enemy's fire. At Anzac, where the confusion appears to have been more pronounced than at Helles, the military situation immediately after the landing was so unfavourable that the withdrawal of the force at nightfall was contemplated by Sir William Birdwood and consequently orders were given to get every wounded man away at once. Surgeon-General Birrell and Lieutenant-Colonel Keble think that some of the confusion might have been avoided if the senior medical officers of the Australian and New Zealand Corps had remained with the headquarters of their divisions, leaving their subordinates to land and do the work on the beaches; and Lieutenant-Colonel Fenwick, DADMS, of the Australian and New Zealand Division, expresses that opinion in regard to his division. Possibly if they had done so they might have been able to exercise better control by being more in touch with the hospital ships, but we do not think that this would have materially affected the situation. In our opinion, the circumstances made confusion inevitable.

The difficulty and confusion mentioned above rapidly decreased after the first few days, and in the operations in August there were few complaints of the arrangements for the removal of the wounded from the beaches and their conveyance to the hospital ships, except on the first day of the fighting at Anzac, when, according to Lieutenant-Colonel Corbin, Medical Officer of the 1st Australian Clearing Station, and Lieutenant-Colonel Begg, Officer Commanding the New Zealand Field Ambulance, there were difficulties from want of transport from the beaches and from the delay in the arrival of two clearing stations which had been provided for that service. This delay was explained by Lieutenant-Colonel Corkery, Officer Commanding the 16th Casualty Clearing Station, one of the two under reference. It does not seem to have been occasioned by any fault in the arrangements of the medical staff.

NEW APPOINTMENTS

At the end of May, Surgeon-General Sir William Babtie was appointed Principal Director of Medical Services in the Mediterranean, and exercised a general supervision over all the medical arrangements for the Mediterranean Expeditionary Force, as well as for Egypt and Malta, Surgeon-General Birrell continuing in the position of Director of Medical Services of the Mediterranean Expeditionary Force until the latter part of August, when he was relieved by Surgeon-General Bedford.

In July, Surgeon-General Sir James Porter was sent out by the Admiralty to superintend the naval and military resources in respect of the sea hospital transport in the Mediterranean, under the title of Principal Hospital Transport Officer (Mediterranean). Up to this time this duty had been performed by

Surgeon-General Birrell and Surgeon-General Ford, under the supervision of Surgeon-General Babtie, though all the movements of the vessels and other craft at sea were under the control of the naval authorities. In consequence of complaints received by Sir Arthur May, the Medical Director-General of the Navy, as to the condition of the wounded afloat and the defective arrangements for the direction of the transports, he represented to Sir Alfred Keogh that it would be well if a naval medical officer were sent out to supervise the shipping arrangements for the sick and wounded. Sir Alfred Keogh agreed to this, and Sir James Porter was accordingly sent out. Sir Ian Hamilton considered that the result would be dual control and consequent confusion, and represented his views to the War Office. Surgeon-General Babtie considered the appointment unnecessary, but he and Sir James Porter worked very well together. Sir James Porter remained there until December, 1915, when his appointment was terminated at the request of the War Office. There is a difference of opinion as to whether any benefit resulted from the appointment. Sir Arthur May thinks that there was an improvement. Sir Alfred Keogh thinks there was not. Vice-Admiral Wemyss told us that from the naval point of view there was a great improvement.

ESTIMATE OF CASUALTIES IN JULY

The question of dealing with casualties became very important in July, in view of the contemplated operations at Helles, Anzac and Suvla, and on July 13th Sir Ian Hamilton informed the War Office that he would need more medical assistance. He pointed out that 20,000 casualties was not an extravagant estimate judging from the results of fighting in the Dardanelles up to that date, and that such a number would require 30 transports converted into temporary hospital ships and 200 extra medical officers, with Royal Army Medical Corps rank-and-file and nurses in proportion.

The contemplated operations first came to the notice of the Director of Medical Services and General Woodward and General Winter at about the same time. Surgeon-General Birrell explained that it was only by accident that he heard of the operations, and that he repeated what he had heard to the other two officers. From another part of his evidence it seems that the telegram mentioned above was sent by Sir Ian Hamilton at his request; and as it did not entirely express what he wanted, another telegram, increasing the demand for orderlies and nurses, was sent. This demand was complied with.

There is the same conflict of evidence as to whether the estimate of the casualties on this occasion was made in the first instance by the General or by the Administrative Staff, but we do not think it necessary to investigate the matter.

Surgeon-General Birrell informed us that his final scheme for the evacuation of casualties from Helles, Anzac, and Suvla was based upon an estimate of 30,000 casualties; and this was also the estimate of

Sir Ian Hamilton, after further considering the question. The scheme provided for the use of six hospital ships and 30 transports used as temporary hospital ships. The hospital ships were to take the serious cases and, when full, carry them to the bases and return to the peninsula. Sir James Porter disapproved of sending the hospital ships away from the battle area, and made out a plan of his own for the movement of the ships and other craft which is set out in his statement. This plan aimed at reserving the hospital ships more exclusively for serious cases and providing greater facilities for separating the light from the serious cases. The cases were then transferred from the hospital ships into transports for carriage to the bases and the hospital ships returned to the beaches.

DIFFICULTIES OF COMMUNICATION

The evacuation was carried out in accordance with Sir James Porter's dispositions and, on the whole, the cases were better sorted than in the original landing, but there was still considerable confusion. This was increased, not only during these operations but throughout the whole time, by the difficulty of communication with, and inspection of, the hospital ships and transports when they arrived at Mudros. The Lines of Communication Staff, including the Deputy Director of Medical Services, were with the naval staff upon the SS *Aragon*, and for the purpose of communication with the shore or with any vessel in the bay, steam or motor launches or boats of some kind were necessary. Of these there was a great deficiency. The military staff on board the *Aragon* were in close touch with the naval authorities, and this advantage would have been lost without any compensating improvement in their means of communication with the vessels in harbour, had their headquarters been established on shore. Evidence to this effect was given by Major-General Altham, the Inspector-General of Communications, and we accept it.

Sir Frederick Treves in his evidence stated that great difficulty was occasioned because the Deputy Director of Medical Services at Mudros had no means of communication with Alexandria or Malta, and therefore did not know what accommodation there was at each place for the wounded, with the result that ships were sent to Alexandria, and then, finding no accommodation there, had to go on to Malta. We think that there is some misunderstanding about this. The statement is inconsistent with the evidence of Vice-Admiral Wemyss, Surgeon-General Birrell, Colonel Keble, Colonel Ryan, and other officers, and with the information given to us by Colonel Maher. Surgeon-General Ford also stated that he could at all times accommodate the wounded sent to him, though at times he sent on slight cases to Malta in order to keep beds available for serious cases.

SICKNESS FROM OTHER CAUSES

In addition to the casualties arising from wounds, there was much sickness, chiefly a form of dysentery and diarrhoea, and large numbers of men had to be removed from the peninsula to hospital. This was especially the case in the height of the summer. At the end of November, 1915, a very severe blizzard occurred, producing numerous cases of frost-bite, and also gangrene from the men's clothing being frozen to their bodies. There was much suffering during this time, and the storm came so suddenly and was so exceptional that no special provision had been made for it.

CONDITIONS ON BOARD THE BLACK SHIPS

We have had much evidence as to the treatment of the sick and wounded during the operations on the Gallipoli Peninsula. Some of it favourable to the medical organisation and arrangements, and some the reverse. The main complaints related to the condition of the wounded on the black ships, and the evidence as to them is contradictory.

Evidence as to the deficiencies of these ships and the consequent suffering of the wounded was given to us by many witnesses, amongst them Rear-Admiral Keyes, Surgeon-General Howse, Lieutenant-Colonel Begg, Fleet-Surgeon Levick, Lieutenant-Colonel Fenwick, Major Kent Hughes, Lieutenant-Colonel Corbin and Lieutenant-Colonel Ryan. Some of the information given to us by these witnesses was given from personal observation and some from reports and communications received by them. It is a subject on which hearsay information should be received with caution, as a natural sympathy with the sufferings of the wounded may lead to some exaggeration.

We think, too, that some of the witnesses have not made sufficient allowance for the inevitable hardships that must attend the evacuation and treatment of casualties under conditions such as existed at Gallipoli.

Colonel Warren Low said that in four or five days at Mudros and Anzac more big operations were performed than the total number performed in the twelve large hospitals in London in a week, and added: "If you are going to expect to have at a place like Anzac all the arrangements one expects at St Thomas's Hospital, you will not get them, and I cannot understand anyone expecting them." Sir Arthur May also said that where there is a very large number of casualties hospital ships cannot be provided for all, and black ships or carriers must be used to a certain extent, and that whenever these are used there must be a large amount of unnecessary suffering. The word "unnecessary" seems to mean suffering which would not result from the wound if treated under favourable conditions.

We think that great importance is to be attached to the evidence of Lieutenant-Colonel Ryan as to the condition of the transports, both because he had had experience of war before this campaign, and because he was Consulting Surgeon and Principal Medical Adviser to General Birdwood at Anzac, and for about a month, from April 25th, was constantly at work on the transports. This is the time during which the state of the transports was at its worst.

According to his [Lieutenant-Colonel Ryan's] evidence, he was on board about ten transports, and in half of them the supply of medical officers was insufficient and there was a want of equipment, such as bed pans, dressings, and clothing for the men. He also describes many of the transports as very dirty, because they had been carrying troops to the peninsula and there was not time to clean them properly. Great difficulty and discomfort was caused in some transports by the fact of horses having been carried on them to Gallipoli. When these ships were selected for the accommodation of wounded it was expected that the horses would have been disembarked before the wounded were put on board, but it was found impossible to disembark them, and on some occasions they were taken several times between Alexandria and Gallipoli. To carry horses and wounded on the same ship must occasion suffering to the latter. Lieutenant-Colonel Ryan stated that he did not think there was much loss of life, but that if all these transports had been fitted up as hospital ships more lives, but not a great many, would have been saved.

We think that this is in substance a fair account of the condition of the transports in the first days of the operations. Lieutenant-Colonel Ryan was only on board one of these transports for a second time and in that case he found a distinct improvement.

Lieutenant-Colonel Ryan also agrees with the evidence of many other witnesses that there was no possibility of separating the wounded into different classes on the beach, and that the cases had to be evacuated as they came without being sorted according to the nature of their wounds.

Sir John Maxwell and Sir Charles McGrigor described the state of the wounded when they arrived at Alexandria as most distressing, and ascribed it to want of medical and nursing attendance; and Lady Carnarvon, who was working amongst the sick at Alexandria, said that the black ships were deficient in nursing staff, and, she believed, in medical staff all the time. General Haggard and Corporal Ross speak of the want of attention and consequent hardships they themselves experienced, and there was other evidence to the same effect.

On the other hand, in answer to a telegram from the War Office of May 10th, 1915:

Representations made here regarding inadequacy of arrangements for wounded. Insufficient doctors, nurses and dressings.

Sir John Maxwell answered, on May 11th, 1915:

Please state the source of representations, which I believe to be unfounded. The rush of wounded could not be dealt with in fitted hospital ships, well supplied with everything, and, therefore, we had to use, and will have to use, ordinary transports. Under most difficult circumstances, the best possible surgical arrangements were made. Of course, as troops had to disembark, and the wounded embark on the same day, the transports could not be cleaned. More than 11,000 cases have been brought from the Dardanelles, all with their wounds dressed. With the exception of 2,000 sent to Malta, all of these were made comfortable in hospital, and within 80 hours of being wounded they were all attended to. The wounded arrived under circumstances well attended to, according to the report of the surgeons in all the hospitals.

Again, on May 23rd, 1915, he telegraphed:

The wounded were all dressed on being put on board, and on arrival were reported by all the medical officers in charge of the hospitals as in a satisfactory condition, taking into consideration the military circumstances under which they were embarked.

This telegram was, apparently, sent after enquiry had been made by Surgeon-General Ford. Surgeon-General Birrell and Surgeon-General Babtie told us that adequate staffs were provided, and, so far as they knew, were on board the ships, though Surgeon-General Birrell admitted that in May the staffs were not sufficient at one time. It is remarkable that this is the time covered by Sir John Maxwell's telegrams.

Lieutenant Colonel Thom, speaking of the time after July 1st, 1915, when he took over the office work of attending to the staffing of the hospital ships and black ships, said that there were always sufficient staffs available at Mudros, and that, so far as he knew, they were on board. Colonel Mayo Robson explained the deficiency of medical and nursing staffs by the fact that serious cases intended for hospital ships were put on the black ships, and he also explained some evidence which was given as to men arriving practically naked by saying that in the summer they fought in that way, and that the sunburnt condition in which they arrived was due to that cause and not to their having been exposed after being wounded, as was supposed by some of the witnesses. Colonel Warren Low also ascribed the condition of the black ships to the difficulties under which the work was done, but he had not much practical experience of those ships. Colonel Sir Courtauld Thomson, Chief Commissioner of the Red Cross Society for Malta, Egypt and the Near East, had the opportunity of seeing many of the black ships, and travelled in some of them. He expressed the opinion that under the exceptional conditions the available resources were utilised to the best advantage.

THE CASE OF THE *SATURNIA*

In some instances transports were used as temporary hospital ships for the reception of wounded at Mudros when the hospital accommodation on shore was fully occupied. This occurred in the case of the *Saturnia*, described by Rear-Admiral Keyes, Fleet-Surgeon Levick and Major Purchas.

According to the evidence given by Major Purchas, Royal Army Medical Corps, he heard on June 29th, soon after his arrival at Mudros from Egypt, that there were a large number of wounded on board the *Saturnia* without sufficient medical attendance. He obtained this information from overhearing a conversation between the captain of the *Minnewaska*, the vessel on which he had come from Egypt, and the captain of another transport. He at once asked for a boat and boarded the *Saturnia*, which he found filled with wounded. At this time, according to his evidence, the only medical officers on board were an Australian medical officer, who had arrived just before him, and Fleet-Surgeon Levick. The latter officer had boarded the *Saturnia* in consequence of a report made to him by a Roman Catholic chaplain that there were a large number of wounded on board the *Saturnia* and only one medical officer.

Soon after Fleet-Surgeon Levick went on board, surgeons from all the ships of the Fleet then lying in harbour were sent to the *Saturnia* in consequence of a general signal. Rear-Admiral Keyes, who took his information from a statement made by Naval Surgeon Lorimer and Fleet-Surgeon Levick, was under the impression that the *Saturnia* had brought these wounded men into Mudros and that the state of their wounds as described by them resulted from neglect on board of her. We see no reason to doubt the evidence of Fleet-Surgeon Levick and Major Purchas that there were a large number of wounded on board the *Saturnia* whose bandages had not been removed since the first dressing and were putrid, and that many of the wounds were in a very foul state and needed prompt attention.

It was not the fact that the *Saturnia* brought the wounded to Mudros from Helles. She was one of four transports taken up in anticipation of the fighting at Helles on June 28th to receive such wounded as could not be accommodated on shore. The other transports were the *Seeang Bee*, the *Minnewaska* and the *Nile*. The *Saturnia* was partly laden with ammunition and could not be used to carry wounded to Egypt, but only for their temporary accommodation at Mudros. The condition of the men's wounds was not produced by neglect on the *Saturnia*, but, according to the evidence of Major Purchas, was the result of the impossibility of bringing them to the dressing stations for some time after they were wounded and their consequent exposure. Major Purchas, however, stated that the condition was aggravated by the want of attention on the *Saturnia*, which he said was quite unprepared and unfitted for their reception. Major Purchas also stated in his evidence that he was informed that the wounded were put on board the *Saturnia* in consequence of a mistaken signal.

On June 30th Colonel Aspinall, who was serving on the General Staff under General Braithwaite, happened to be at Mudros and reported to General Headquarters at Imbros as follows:

> I was informed at Mudros yesterday that 1,350 wounded, including a large proportion of stretcher

cases, had arrived there in fleet sweepers and trawlers, including Isle of Man paddle steamers. Two hundred and fifty additional cases arrived during the day in similar ships. There was insufficient accommodation for these men on arrival, with the result that 600 cases were yesterday morning transferred to the ammunition ship *Saturnia*. Yesterday afternoon it was reported to the naval authorities by the Roman Catholic chaplain that there were 800 sick and wounded on the *Saturnia* and only two doctors to look after them. Admiral Wemyss accordingly ordered each man-of-war in harbour to send a surgeon on board.

This report on receipt at General Headquarters was referred to Surgeon-General Birrell, who the next day, July 1st, sent Colonel Keble to Mudros to enquire into the matter. Colonel Maher was at that time Deputy Director of Medical Services on the Lines of Communication at Mudros, and was responsible under the Director of Medical Services, who was at Imbros, for the medical arrangements at Mudros. Colonel Keble stated in evidence that on reaching Mudros he was informed by Colonel Maher that the wounded had been put on board the *Saturnia* by the mistake of the master of a fleet sweeper, and that they had been removed as soon as Colonel Maher heard of it. Colonel Keble did not make any further enquiry. Having regard to the specific allegations in Colonel Aspinall's report it appears to us that Colonel Keble's enquiry was perfunctory and insufficient.

We think that the evidence establishes that the wounded were put on board at some time on June 29th and that they were removed, some on June 30th to the *Nile* and the remainder on July 1st to the *Minnewaska*, both of which were properly fitted to receive them.

Major Purchas stated that on June 30th he was not in want of more medical assistance.

It is difficult to be certain as to the number of wounded on the *Saturnia*, but we think Major Purchas's evidence is probably correct. He stated the number as about 800, and as he was in charge of their removal from the *Saturnia* to the *Nile* and the *Minnewaska*, and was afterwards in charge of the *Minnewaska* while taking those transferred to that ship from Mudros to Alexandria, he had good opportunities of estimating the number.

After hearing the evidence of Fleet-Surgeon Levick and Major Purchas, we at once communicated with Colonel Maher. He is at present on duty with the Egyptian Expeditionary Force and has not given evidence before us, but we caused enquiries to be made from him by cable as to circumstances connected with the *Saturnia*. His answer is in direct contradiction of most of the evidence stated above. It is in substance as follows:

When the fighting on June 28th was anticipated he was told to expect a certain number of wounded, and took up and got ready the transports already mentioned for their reception. It was intended that the more serious cases should be put on board the hospital ships at Helles, only the less serious being brought to Mudros. By some mistake at Helles, many cases intended for the hospital ships were not put on board of them, but were brought to Mudros, and more accommodation than had been contemplated was required at that place. When the accommodation on shore was exhausted it was necessary to put the wounded on board the transports mentioned, and he ordered some of them to be put on board the *Saturnia*. Only 300 cases were put on board of her, and eight military medical officers and other medical personnel with medical and surgical equipments were put on board at once. The wounded were not left without sufficient medical attention, and help was given on this, as on many other occasions, by naval surgeons. On June 30th all the serious cases were transferred to the *Nile*, and on July 1st the remainder were transferred to the *Minnewaska*. Colonel Maher also stated that on June 29th and 30th he went on board the *Saturnia* and satisfied himself that the sick were well cared for.

Towards the end of August, 1915, in consequence of a complaint made to the War Office about the treatment of the wounded on board the *Saturnia*, Colonel Maher sent a report to Surgeon-General Babtie, the Principal Director of Medical Services in the Mediterranean, in which he gave substantially the same account of the circumstances as that contained in his cable sent in answer to our enquiry. He also stated that Major Purchas, an Australian surgeon of wide experience, was in charge and was assisted by several other competent surgeons. Major Purchas, in fact, comes from New Zealand and not from Australia. It appears from War Office records that Surgeon-General Babtie informed the War Office on August 31st that he had personally visited the *Saturnia* on July 1st, and that on that day there were eight medical officers on board, while a number of naval medical officers were also assisting as voluntary helpers. He stated that the number of wounded on board was about 500 and that the *Saturnia* was quite a suitable ship for the purpose to which she was put, but could not be used as a carrier, as she was loaded with ammunition.

We must point out, however, that on July 1st all the more serious cases had been removed to the *Nile* and medical and other assistance had been obtained, so that Surgeon-General Babtie's statement is no guide to the state of things on June 29th. His statement of the number of cases then on board as 500 is more consistent with Major Purchas's estimate of number than with Colonel Maher's statement that only 300 were put on board.

We are of the opinion that no definite conclusion can be formed on this matter in the absence of the evidence of Colonel Maher and any witnesses whom he might wish to be called. Colonel Maher is at present on active service with the Egyptian Expeditionary Force. We have communicated with the War Office and are informed that for military reasons the Army Council strongly deprecate the recall of Colonel Maher to England at the present time.

Under these circumstances, in order fully to investigate the matter, it would be necessary to postpone the presentation of our report for an indefinite period. We do not feel justified in taking such a course, as a decision upon this particular incident would not affect the general conclusions at which we have arrived on the medical arrangements.

In view, however, of the serious nature of the evidence recorded in the present case, especially as affecting the conduct and capacity of Colonel Maher, we recommend that, as soon as the exigencies of the public service permit, steps should be taken by the Army Council definitely to ascertain with whom the responsibility rests for the deplorable state of things which has been represented to us as existing on board the *Saturnia* on June 29th.

SUMMARY

As regards the medical arrangements generally, although the evidence in several material respects is conflicting, we consider that a fair inference to be drawn from it is that much suffering was caused to the wounded during their evacuation from the peninsula, and that some part of it might have been avoided. Much of this suffering and discomfort was occasioned by the use of the black ships for serious cases. This, in our opinion, arose not so much from a miscalculation of the actual number of casualties as from a miscalculation of the circumstances under which they would be handled. All arrangements were made on the assumption that much more ground would be gained, that the hospitals would be landed, and that there would be an opportunity of sorting the casualties which did not exist on beaches constantly under fire. The difficulties which arose in evacuating the wounded were largely due to an under-estimate of the opposition which would be encountered, and too confident an anticipation of rapid and substantial success. The conditions on shore were, as we have said, aggravated by the impossibility of any proper inspection and regulation of the ships at Mudros by reason of the want of facilities of communication.

Though a great deal of discomfort, amounting in many cases to actual suffering, was occasioned to the wounded by the deficiency in medical attendance and the want of proper appliances on board the transports, we think that the result of the evidence is that the loss of life in consequence was small.

In our opinion, most of the suffering was due to the causes here mentioned, but we also think that there was, in some instances, a lack of organisation and supervision. Evidence of this was given by Admiral Keyes, Major Kent Hughes, and Surgeon-General Howse. The last-named witness described the conditions as "extremely difficult" and exceptional, and said: "We were in the unfortunate position of having no history to guide us of a previous landing on such a large scale in modern times, so that we could get no idea of what medical arrangements should have been made." We think that many of the difficulties might have been avoided if a general plan of the operations had been carefully worked out before the expedition was undertaken.

Many of the wounded after evacuation were taken to hospitals in Egypt and at Malta, and others were sent to England, Australia, New Zealand, or India. We consider the hospitals in England, Australia, New Zealand, and India to be outside the scope of our enquiry. We had some evidence laid before us as to the condition of the hospitals in Egypt and Malta, but we do not propose to discuss it at any length. Our conclusion is that, though there may have been some difficulties at first, especially in Egypt, which were the inevitable result of the large development of hospital accommodation, the provision and management of the hospitals were, under the circumstances, satisfactory. At times stores were not readily obtainable, but this resulted from the general difficulties of transport, and not from anything specially connected with the medical arrangements.

There were also hospitals for the lighter cases established at Mudros and Imbros. At Mudros their establishment was hampered by the want of piers and roads and other facilities of a port; and at one time, in order to be near the landing places and the water supply, the hospitals were placed too near to the general camp, but this was afterwards rectified. There was also evidence that the ground on which the hospitals stood became infected, and that they should have been moved on that account. On this subject there seems to be a difference of opinion. On the whole, we think that the position of the hospitals at Mudros is fairly described by Surgeon-General Babtie. The effect of this evidence is that at first there was not sufficient accommodation and, owing to the absence of water, roads and piers, its provision was very difficult; but that, as the size of the force increased, the supply of medical officers and attendants increased in proportion. It is possible that from time to time there was a shortage of medical attendance, but we do not think it existed to any serious extent.

When the weather became hot, there was a great increase of sickness, chiefly dysentery, diarrhoea, and para-typhoid, and these diseases were carried by the enormous number of flies. It was, therefore, very important that the sanitation of the camps and trenches should be properly carried out. On the whole, so far as conditions permitted, we think this was done. Surgeon-General Babtie states that the difficulties in remedying defects were almost insuperable owing to the cramped positions held and the lack of materials, such as wood and corrugated iron to enclose the latrines and make them fly-proof and to provide fly-proof kitchen-shelters. Some materials sent for the purpose were lost or damaged by accident of war, but one of the main causes of the deficiency was the anticipation that the operations would be very short, and the consequent omission to make provision for a long occupation of the peninsula.

Effective sanitation of the whole area was made impossible by the fact that our trenches were very near to those of the Turks, who took no sanitary measures at all. In July, a Sanitary Advisory Committee was appointed, which arrived in the peninsula after the fighting in August. The members of this Committee were all men of acknowledged scientific position, and their reports were of great service. A bacteriological laboratory was established at Mudros, and did good work.

There does not seem to be any complaint as to the supply of medicine, except in the case of Australian and New Zealand troops, who were said to have been short of the ordinary medicines, especially castor oil, and of the variety of food required for men suffering from illness. There is no dispute as to the fact that, at one time, the supply of castor oil ran short, the explanation put forward being that the supply was sufficient to meet ordinary demands, but that for some reason these troops required and consumed more drugs than the normal supply. This is probably correct, for there are no complaints of a lack of drugs in any other quarter.

POSTAL ARRANGEMENTS

The postal arrangements for letters and parcels sent to the Mediterranean Expeditionary Force were complicated, and increased in difficulty as the number of troops increased. The arrangements also changed from time to time. The statements of Lieutenant-Colonel Williamson, Director of Army Postal Service, Major McClintock, Director Army Postal Service Mediterranean Expeditionary Force, and Captain McCurdy, Officer Commanding New Zealand Base

Post Office, set out all the details of the system, and will be found elsewhere.

Various complaints as to the service were brought before us. They were chiefly concerned with the non-delivery or late delivery of letters and parcels to the New Zealand troops, but we think what happened with regard to them may be taken as fairly representing the facts as to the whole of the force. The only material difference is that the mails for the New Zealand troops were passed through a very efficient New Zealand Post Office under Captain McCurdy, but they remained always under the control of the General Post Office.

Complaints were made by General R. P. Maxwell, General Cox and Colonel Mayo Robson.

The two former complained that parcels regularly despatched from England were only delivered in rare instances, and the latter that letters addressed to him were delivered on board the *Aragon*, where the Naval and part of the Administrative Staff were quartered. Colonel Mayo Robson on more than one occasion went on board and asked for his letters, and was told there were none for him, and eventually they were all found in the hold in another part of the *Aragon*. He said they consisted of letters and newspapers extending over a period from July to October, 1915, and contained several orders which had been sent to him by Surgeon-General Babtie and others. We have not been able to get any explanation of this incident. The letters had been carried and delivered at the place to which they were addressed and, in the absence of explanation, we can only conclude that it was owing to the negligence or stupidity of some postal clerk on board the *Aragon* that they were not given to Colonel Mayo Robson.

It must be remembered that the Post Office was not the only agency by which parcels were sent to the Mediterranean Expeditionary Force. A great many were sent by the Army Service Corps Parcels Transit Service, and the Post Office was sometimes held responsible for the delay or non-delivery of parcels which were not entrusted to them. Speaking generally, parcels up to 11 lbs were sent by post and parcels above that weight by the military forwarding office. There was a good deal of looting of parcels sent by the military forwarding office, probably because they were not sent in sealed bags, as Post Office parcels were.

Still, it cannot be doubted that there were delays and failures in the delivery of letters and parcels which were sent by the Post Office. In considering the amount of blame, if any, to be attached to the department, it is necessary not to lose sight of two main considerations.

(1) The number of letters and parcels was very large, and increased very rapidly, and a failure to deliver a very small percentage of the letters and parcels would amount to a formidable figure and give rise to many complaints. The amount of letters is stated to have grown to 1,000,000 a week, and the parcels are variously stated as from 40,000 or 90,000 a week. The difference is prob-

ably accounted for by a difference in the estimate of the number of parcels to a bag.

(2) The service was performed under circumstances of great difficulty, and for this reason the delivery of mails cannot fairly be compared with delivery in ordinary circumstances or to the troops in France.

The system of checking the bags was elaborate and efficient, as is shown by the fact that every bag except one could be traced and accounted for, and that cases in which the bags had been tampered with were also discovered. This checking continued up to the time when the mails were delivered to the post orderlies of the different units. After they had been so delivered the responsibility of the Post Office ceased.

In consequence of complaints as to the postal service, Colonel Williamson was sent out specially to make enquiries and report, which he did in October, 1915. His report is substantially in accordance with the evidence of other witnesses.

From this report it appears that the Post Office probably had to bear some of the responsibility which properly attached to the Army Service Corps Parcels Transit Service as well as its own.

The Post Office sent the letters via Marseilles and the parcels by P&O packets from the Thames. The result was that a letter advising the despatch of a parcel often arrived a considerable time before the parcel, and complaints were made of its non-arrival because the addressee of the letter did not appreciate that they were not sent together.

In cases where the addressee had become a casualty or for some other reason was not with his unit, there were great difficulties in finding where he was and in delivering his letters or parcels, even if they arrived safe and were not distributed to other men. The names of several men whose letters were not delivered were supplied to us by the Office of the High Commissioner of New Zealand. These cases were investigated so far as was possible by Captain McCurdy, and the result is given by him in his statement. They illustrate the difficulty experienced in delivering mails when the addressees were not with their unit.

Many parcels were destroyed through insufficient packing. The bags were handled and transhipped several times, and could not always be carefully handled, the result being that parcels were burst open and their contents crushed so as to be quite indistinguishable. Colonel Williamson described in his evidence the state of a large number of bags of parcels which had been sent up to the Front and returned to Alexandria because they could not be delivered. He says:

> The state in which these parcels arrived was absolutely deplorable. It was a deplorable sight. There was hardly a vestige of a resemblance to a parcel left. The contents were often ground to powder. The packing was all gone, the address was illegible, and one would simply get a bagful of *disjecta membra* [dismembered objects] of a parcel which it was impossible to reassemble and send on. That must have accounted for a very large proportion.

It is improbable that all this damage was done on their return from the Front to Alexandria, and it may therefore be concluded that many parcels arrived at the Front in the state described by Colonel Williamson. In many cases where the addressee was not present with his unit, the parcels, rightly or wrongly, were treated as common property, and distributed amongst his comrades.

In the case of letters which arrived at intervals over a considerable period and were not delivered as they arrived, but all together at a later date, the fault may have been that of the unit to which the addressee belonged and not that of the Post Office, whose duty was discharged when the letter was delivered to the post orderly. In one case that was investigated by Captain McCurdy this proved to have been the case. It does not seem to have been so in the case of Colonel Mayo Robson.

Parcels sent to General Cox were packed by the Army and Navy Stores and forwarded by Parcel Post. Presumably, they would be properly packed. We have not been able to ascertain anything further with regard to this case or that of General Maxwell.

The causes mentioned above account for a very large proportion of the complaints, but they do not explain them all. There must have been cases in which the Post Office was at fault. Considering the difficulties of the service and the amount of letters and parcels which had to be handled, we think that some miscarriage was inevitable, and we are of opinion that, on the whole, no blame attaches to those responsible for the organization and conduct of the service.

THE ZION MULE CORPS

The Zion Mule Corps was raised in Alexandria from a number of Jewish refugees from Syria. They or their fathers had gone to Syria following the principle of Zionism and at the outbreak of war they came to Egypt and were under the charge of a Mr Hornblower, Inspector of Refugees in the Ministry of the Interior, Egypt. The Corps, when raised, was put under the command of Lieutenant-Colonel Patterson, and did good work in Gallipoli as a transport Corps.

The only question raised before us was as to the terms of service and pension on which they were engaged. We doubt if this question is strictly within our reference, but we think it well to represent the facts as stated to us. Evidence was given to us by Lieutenant-Colonel Patterson and Captain Trumpeldor. Lieutenant-Colonel Patterson spoke in a great measure from hearsay, and the important evidence was that of Captain Trumpeldor. We consider him quite a trustworthy witness.

Lieutenant-Colonel Patterson said that there were two meetings held at which officials of the British Government addressed the men and told them that they would be treated in all respects in the same way as British soldiers and would receive the same pay and everything else, and that the men agreed to serve in the Corps on those terms.

Captain Trumpeldor said that they wished to raise a fighting unit to fight for Palestine and the Zion ideal, and did not want to serve as a transport unit because they did not think it so honourable. He said that he and a committee of prominent Israelites saw Sir John Maxwell and discussed the question of forming a fighting or a transport unit, and that afterwards a meeting of the men was held at which they were addressed by Mr Hornblower and a staff officer who spoke in Sir John Maxwell's name. This staff officer was Captain (now Lieutenant Colonel) H. V. Holdich, DSO.

According to Captain Trumpeldor's evidence the men were told by Mr Hornblower and Captain

Holdich that a transport and a fighting unit in the British Army were equally honourable and served on the same conditions. Some of the men who were married and had families asked what would happen to their families if they were killed or wounded, and in answer they were told that like the families of soldiers they would receive a pension and allowance. Captain Trumpeldor said that he did not remember the expression "pensions" being used, as Mr Hornblower and Captain Holdich spoke in English and he did not understand it very well, but that what they said was translated into Hebrew by Mr Gordon, a clerk in Mr Hornblower's office. Captain Trumpeldor spoke English fairly well and gave his evidence in English.

Lieutenant-Colonel Holdich is on active service in Egypt. We made enquiries from him by telegraph, and received an answer that to the best of his recollection no mention specifically was made of any gratuities or pensions, as it was understood that any question regarding them would be settled later by the General Officer Commanding-in-Chief of the Mediterranean Force, according to the nature of the work on which the Corps was employed; and that he believes an agreement was made between Sir J. Maxwell and the General Officer Commanding-in-Chief of the Mediterranean Force. He also stated that the terms, so far as he made them, were defined in writing to the War Office in a letter at the beginning of April, 1915, as 1s. a day and khaki uniform, without any other conditions. The letter mentioned is one from Sir John Maxwell, of April 10th, 1915. The War Office have not been able to find it, but we are informed by General Headquarters in Egypt that it contained no mention of gratuities or pensions.

We referred Captain Trumpeldor's evidence to Sir John Maxwell and received in answer a letter in which he stated:

> My staff officer was Captain [now Lieutenant-Colonel] Holdich, DSO, and he drew up the terms of service. As far as my recollection goes Colonel Patterson has correctly stated the case. The terms of service of the men must be available in Egypt; they accepted the conditions and were taken on the strength of the Mediterranean Expeditionary Force.

On receiving this letter we communicated with Lieutenant-Colonel Holdich, and received the answer mentioned above.

Some of the Corps were killed and wounded, and a question as to the payment of pensions arose. In August, 1915, Sir John Maxwell wrote to the War Office:

> Although no promise or agreement of any sort was made regarding pensions, the men were evidently quite under the impression that in case of their death, pensions or compensation of some sort would be granted to their widows.

He recommended the payment of a gratuity in lieu of a pension, owing to the difficulties that might arise in the payment of pensions.

In September, 1915, he again wrote to the War Office and explained that the men were not attested [enlisted], but had entered into a voluntary agreement to serve at the pay of 1s. a day, their families being maintained in refuge camps during their absence. He concluded: "No authorised mention of pension was made to them before joining, but they undoubtedly consider themselves eligible for the same consideration as soldiers," and again recommended gratuities rather than pensions.

Authority has been obtained from the Treasury to issue gratuities to the Zion Mule Corps men if disabled or to their dependants if they die.

Some of the men sent a petition to Lieutenant-Colonel Patterson complaining that they only received gratuities instead of pensions, and said that it was not fair after what had been said to them when they joined.

We suggest for the favourable consideration of the War Office the question whether, under the circumstances, the men of this Corps should not be treated as to pensions similarly to British soldiers regularly enlisted.

GENERAL REVIEW

Before setting out the conclusions to which we have come, it seems desirable briefly to review the salient features of the Dardanelles Expedition in their broad military aspect. We would first refer to the paper on the possibility of a joint naval and military attack upon the Dardanelles, drawn up by the General Staff at the War Office for the consideration of the Committee of Imperial Defence and dated December 19th, 1906, in which the following statement appears:

The successful conclusion of a military enterprise directed against the Gallipoli Peninsula must hinge upon the ability of the Fleet not only to dominate the Turkish defences with gun fire, and crush their field troops during that period of helplessness which exists while an army is in actual process of disembarkation, but also to cover the advance of the troops once ashore until they could gain a firm foothold, and establish themselves upon the high ground in rear of the coast defences of the Dardanelles. However brilliant as a combination of war and, however fruitful in its consequences such an operation would be, were it crowned with success, the General Staff, in view of the risks involved, are not prepared to recommend its being attempted.

These words were written before the recent development of deep trenches flanked by hidden machine guns, concealed howitzer batteries, and the other appliances of modern defensive warfare. Sir John de Robeck pointed out to Sir Ian Hamilton at their first interview on March 17th, 1915, that the peninsula was rapidly being fortified, that all the landing places were now defended by lines of trenches and effectively commanded by field guns and howitzers which could not be located from the sea, that the Turks possessed searchlights of the latest pattern which were skilfully handled, and that their troops were so ably disposed and heavily entrenched that they had not much to fear from the flat trajectory guns of the Navy. Sir John de Robeck subsequently sent a telegram on May 9th, 1915, to the Admiralty, in which he remarked:

> The Navy is of small assistance when it is a matter of trenches and machine guns, and the check of the Army is due to these factors.

It will be seen that the condition which the General Staff had laid down in 1906 as being essential to the success of a military enterprise on the Gallipoli Peninsula was incapable of fulfilment; and though Sir John de Robeck's views about naval gunfire were of great importance, we cannot find that they were taken into serious consideration or communicated to the War Office.

Landings took place at Helles and Anzac with disappointing results. The troops not only suffered heavy loss during disembarkation, but subsequently were unable to advance beyond a short distance from the beach, or to establish themselves on the high ground which the Turks had occupied and entrenched. Our forces on the peninsula were in the position of isolated garrisons confined to small areas on the fringe of the shore, and engaged in trench warfare against an enemy possessing freedom of movement, advantages of ground, and the power of concentration and rapid reinforcement. Our garrisons fought bravely and lost heavily, but were unable to make any substantial advance.

Sir Ian Hamilton made an effort to extricate his troops from the trench warfare in which they were entangled by means of the combined operations at the beginning of August. These operations failed, partly because the Turks were too strong, partly because some of our troops and their leaders were unequal to the task assigned them, partly through shortage of water, and partly because the plan was defective. The descriptions of the ground on the northern and north-western slopes of Sari Bahr, and of the hills to the north and east of Suvla Bay, lead us to the conclusion that in the plan of operations too little importance was attached to natural difficulties. We doubt whether it was prudent or advantageous to order night advances through so difficult a country, especially when no complete preliminary reconnaissance had been or could have been made. In hardly any case, either at Anzac or Suvla, were the troops able to reach the specified objectives at or near the time mentioned in the plan.

Thus from the beginning the execution of the plan was delayed, and this delay caused a loss of cohesion and co-operation among the attacking units. In spite of heat, want of water and difficulties of ground, the troops with very few exceptions appear to have fought well and in some instances heroically; but after successive nights and days of strenuous effort they became exhausted and in urgent need of rest and reorganisation. The losses, too, had been so heavy that without large reinforcements nothing further could be attempted. Even with large reinforcements it had become increasingly evident that no substantial success could be achieved without an overwhelming preponderance of high angle and high explosive fire upon the Turkish entrenchments which confronted our positions on the shore.

Viewed as a military enterprise which was undertaken not as a surprise, but after ample warning had been given to the enemy of the probability of a land attack, we are of the opinion that from the outset the risks of failure attending the expedition outweighed its chances of success. The conditions of the problem, so far as we can judge, were not fully investigated in the first instance by competent experts, and no correct appreciation of the nature and difficulties of the task involved was arrived at. In the absence of such appreciation the authorities responsible for the expedition confidently expected that military action on the peninsula would be short and decisive and, that after the Turkish defences had been destroyed and the Turkish guns dismounted, the force which had been landed would be available for such operations in the vicinity of Constantinople as might seem appropriate.

The strength of the opposition to our landing on the peninsula and the failure of our troops to make any material impression on the Turkish entrenchments which hemmed them in came, therefore, as a surprise. The heavy losses and the repeated checks that were experienced up to the end of July caused the authorities considerable anxiety, but they were naturally reluctant to abandon a project, the realisation of which would have had such far-reaching effects. The failure of the combined attack early in August, from which much had been hoped and for which large reinforcements had been despatched from England, was a severe disappointment to the Government and the country. Doubts arose as to the ultimate success of the expedition, and alternative courses of action came under consideration. It was open to the Government, if the requisite resources in the way of men, guns, and munitions were forthcoming, promptly to strengthen the Expeditionary Force to such an extent as would enable it to drive the Turks out of the peninsula, or at least to attempt to do so. Or our garrisons on the shore of the peninsula might be maintained in the positions they were then occupying until the spring of 1916, provided that the Turks did not bring heavy guns into play and render these positions untenable; or steps might be taken for the evacuation of the peninsula before the winter set in.

There was much divergence of opinion in regard to these different courses, the General Staff at the War Office, which by this time was in process of resuscitation, being strongly in favour of evacuation. To Sir Ian Hamilton such a step as evacuation was unthinkable, and he informed Lord Kitchener accordingly. On October 11th Lord Kitchener also told the Dardanelles Committee that in his opinion the abandonment of the Gallipoli Peninsula would be disastrous. On the other hand, Sir Charles Monro strongly urged its expediency and feasibility, and this view, though at first distasteful to Lord Kitchener, was afterwards accepted by him. At last the Government resolved to withdraw from the peninsula. We think that this was a wise and courageous decision. It was generally recognised that the evacuation would in all probability involve heavy loss in men and material. Besides this, stress had been laid on the irreparable damage to our prestige in the Eastern world which would attend our abandonment of the expedition. Fortunately, however, in the result our losses proved to be inappreciable and hitherto our prestige appears to have remained unimpaired.

It has been represented in some of the evidence which has come before us that from a military point of view the Dardanelles Expedition, even if unsuccessful, was justified by the fact that it neutralised or contained a large number of Turkish troops who otherwise would have been free to operate elsewhere. Lord Kitchener estimated this number as being nearly 300,000. But in containing the Turkish force we employed on the peninsula and at Lemnos and Imbros 385,700 officers and soldiers, besides Indian soldiers—a total of at least 400,000. Our casualties amounted to 31,389 killed, 78,749 wounded and 9,708 missing, making a total of 119,846. The expedition also involved heavy financial expenditure and the employment of a considerable naval force and of a large amount of merchant shipping.

Taking these factors into consideration, we do not think that from a military standpoint our gain in one direction compensated for our losses in other directions. On the other hand, certain important political advantages were secured.

Our attention has been called to the fact that in our First Report,★ we quoted an extract from a statement made to us by Mr Churchill in which he referred to the changed attitude of Lord Fisher towards the operations at the Dardanelles. Mr Churchill's statement was in fact given as relating not to the period "shortly after January 13th" but to a much later period.

While we gladly make this correction, we wish to add that the conclusions stated are in our opinion established by the evidence and are in no way vitiated [undermined] by this correction.

We regret that the official duties of Mr Fisher as High Commissioner of Australia became latterly so exacting as to deprive us to a large extent of his help. For this reason, as explained in his separate memorandum, he considers it inadvisable to sign the report.

It will be noticed that Sir Thomas Mackenzie has added a memorandum dealing with certain aspects of the Enquiry on which he takes a stronger view than the general body of the Commissioners.

★ See *Lord Kitchener and Winston Churchill: the Dardanelles Commission Part I* in the Uncovered Editions series.

GENERAL CONCLUSIONS

We think that, when it was decided to undertake an important military expedition to the Gallipoli Peninsula, sufficient consideration was not given to the measures necessary to carry out such an expedition with success. We have already pointed out that it had been apparent in February, 1915, that serious military operations might be necessary. Under these circumstances we think that the conditions of a military attack on the peninsula should have been studied and a general plan prepared by the Chief of the Imperial General Staff, Sir James Wolfe Murray, special attention being paid to the probable effect of naval gun-fire in support of the troops; and that it was the duty of the Secretary of State for War to ensure that this was done.

We think that the difficulties of the operations were much underestimated. At the outset all decisions were taken and all provisions based on the assumption that, if a landing were effected, the resistance would be slight and the advance rapid. We can see no sufficient ground for this assumption. The short naval bombardment in November, 1914, had given the Turks warning of a possible attack, and the naval operations in February and March of 1915 led naturally to a great strengthening of the Turkish defences. The Turks were known to be led by German officers, and there was no reason to think that they would not fight well, especially in defensive positions. These facts had been reported by Admiral de Robeck and Sir Ian Hamilton.

We think that the position which, in fact, existed after the first attacks in April and the early days of May should have been regarded from the outset as possible and the requisite means of meeting it considered. This would have made it necessary to examine and decide whether the demands of such extended operations could be met consistently with our obligations in other theatres of war. In fact those obligations made it impossible in May, June, and July to supply the forces with the necessary drafts, gun ammunition, high explosives and other modern appliances of war.

We are of the opinion that, with the resources then available, success in the Dardanelles, if possible, was only possible upon condition that the Government concentrated their efforts upon the enterprise and limited their expenditure of men and material in the Western theatre of war. This condition was never fulfilled.

After the failure of the attacks which followed the first landing there was undue delay in deciding upon the course to be pursued in the future. Sir Ian Hamilton's appreciation was forwarded on May 17th, 1915. It was not considered by the War Council or the Cabinet until June 7th. The reconstruction of the Government which took place at this most critical period was the main cause of the delay. As a consequence the despatch of the reinforcements asked for by Sir Ian Hamilton in his appreciation was postponed for six weeks.

We think that the plan of attack from Anzac and Suvla in the beginning of August was open to criticism. The country over which the attack had to be made was very difficult, especially at Anzac. In order to obtain if possible the element of surprise, the main advance of the Anzac force up the north-western spurs of Sari Bahr was undertaken at night, the risk of misdirection and failure being much increased thereby. The plan, however, was decided upon after a consideration of other plans, and with the concurrence of the Commander of the Anzac Corps, who had been in command since the first landing.

The operations at Suvla were a severe trial for a force consisting of troops who had never been under fire, but we think that after taking into consideration and making every allowance for the difficulties of the attack and the inexperience of the troops, the attack was not pressed as it should have been at Suvla on the 7th and 8th August, and we attribute this in a great measure to a want of determination and competence in the Divisional Commander and one of his Brigadiers. The leading of the 11th Division and the attached battalions of the 10th Division, which constituted the main body of the attack, was not satisfactory. As explained previously, the orders given by General Hammersley were confused and the work of his staff defective. Major-General Hammersley's health had in the past been such that it was dangerous to select him for a divisional command in the field, although he seemed to have recovered. We think that the defects that we have mentioned in his leading probably arose from this cause. General Sitwell, the senior Brigade Commander, did not, in our opinion, show sufficient energy and decision.

Sir Frederick Stopford was hampered by the want of effective leadership referred to above, and the inexperience of his troops, but we do not think he took sufficient means to inform himself of the progress of operations. On August 7th, when he became aware that the troops had not advanced as rapidly as had been intended, we think that he should have asked for some explanation from General Hammersley. In that case he would have been informed of the difference which had arisen between General Sitwell and General Hill, and of General Sitwell's lack of vigour and energy in leading. We think that at this point his intervention was needed.

We think that he and his staff were partly responsible for the failure to supply the troops with water on August 7th and 8th. Our detailed conclusions on the water supply will be found below.

We cannot endorse Sir Ian Hamilton's condemnation of the orders given by Sir Frederick Stopford on the morning of August 8th, 1915, whether the account of them given in Sir Ian Hamilton's despatch or that in Sir Frederick Stopford's report to him be accepted. According to the evidence of Sir Bryan Mahon and General Hammersley, they were not deterred from advancing by those orders.

On the evening of August 8th we think that Sir Frederick Stopford's difficulties were increased by the intervention of Sir Ian Hamilton. Sir Ian Hamilton seems to have considered Sir Frederick Stopford lacking in energy in the operations between August 9th and August 15th. As this opinion is based more upon general conduct than upon any specific acts or omissions, we are not in a position to pronounce upon it. We realise, however, that importance attaches to the impressions of a Commander-in-Chief on such a subject.

As regards Sir Ian Hamilton it is inevitable that the capabilities of a commander in war should be judged by the results he achieves, even though, if these results are disappointing, his failure may be due to causes for which he is only partially responsible.

In April, 1915, Sir Ian Hamilton succeeded in landing his troops at the places which he had chosen; but the operations that were intended immediately to follow the landing were abruptly checked owing to a miscalculation of the strength of the Turkish defences and the fighting qualities of the Turkish troops. This rebuff should have convinced Sir Ian Hamilton that the Turkish entrenchments were skilfully disposed and well armed, and that naval gun-fire was ineffective against trenches and entanglements of the modern type. We doubt, however, whether the failure of these operations sufficiently impressed Sir Ian Hamilton and the military authorities at home with the serious nature of the opposition likely to be encountered.

During May, June, and July severe fighting took place, but its results were not commensurate with the efforts made and the losses incurred.

During July a plan of combined operations was elaborated, which was carried into effect early in August. Sir Ian Hamilton was confident of success, but was again baffled by the obstinacy of the Turkish resistance. Moreover, the failure of night advances in a difficult and unexplored country, which formed part of the plan, led to heavy casualties and temporarily disorganised the forces employed.

Sir Ian Hamilton was relieved of his command on October 15th.

We recognise Sir Ian Hamilton's personal gallantry and energy, his sanguine disposition, and his determination to win at all costs. We recognise also that the task entrusted to him was one of extreme difficulty, the more so as the authorities at home at first misconceived the nature and duration of the operations, and afterwards were slow to realise that to drive the Turks out of their entrenchments and occupy the heights commanding the Straits was a formidable and hazardous enterprise which demanded a concentration of force and effort. It must further be borne in mind that Lord Kitchener, whom Sir Ian Hamilton appears to have regarded as a Commander-in-Chief rather than as a Secretary of State, pressed upon him the paramount importance, if it were by any means possible, of carrying out the task assigned to him.

Though from time to time Sir Ian Hamilton represented the need of drafts, reinforcements, guns and munitions, which the Government found it impossible to supply, he was nevertheless always ready to renew the struggle with the resources at his disposal, and to the last was confident of success. For this it would be hard to blame him; but viewing the expedition in the light of events it would, in our opinion, have been well had he examined the situation as disclosed by the first landings in a more critical spirit, impartially weighed the probabilities of success and failure, having regard to the resources in men and material which could be placed at his disposal, and submitted to the Secretary of State for War a comprehensive statement of the arguments for and against a continuance of the operations.

The failure at Anzac was due mainly to the difficulties of the country and the strength of the enemy. The failure at Suvla also prevented any pressure being put upon the Turkish force in that direction, and success at Suvla might have lessened the resistance at Anzac.

We think that after the attacks ending on August 9th had failed, the operations contemplated could not have been successfully carried out without large reinforcements. The fighting after General de Lisle replaced Sir Frederick Stopford was really of a defensive character.

We think that after the advice of Sir Charles Monro had been confirmed by Lord Kitchener the decision to evacuate should have been taken at once. We recognise, however, that the question of evacuation was connected with other questions of high policy which do not appear to us to come within the scope of our enquiry.

We think that the decision to evacuate when taken was right.

We think that the operations were hampered throughout by the failure to supply sufficient artillery and munitions, and to keep the original formations up to strength by the provision of adequate drafts as well as reinforcements. In our opinion this was not owing to any neglect on the part of the Heads of Departments charged with such provision, but to the demands proving much larger than was expected when the operations were undertaken and to demands which had to be met in other theatres of war.

On the other hand, a considerable amount of artillery was available in Egypt and at Mudros for the Suvla operations, but it was not utilised.

Many minor frontal attacks were made without adequate artillery preparation, which produced little or no material advantage. Evidence was given that these attacks entailed an unnecessary loss of life. Without a more intimate knowledge of the locality and conditions than it is possible for us to obtain, we cannot express an opinion as to whether it was right to undertake such attacks. We think that the evidence disproves the allegation made before us that useless attacks were made because of the neglect on the part of superior commanders and staff officers to visit and inspect the trenches and positions.

There was full co-operation between the Navy and Army and the two services worked well and harmoniously together.

CONCLUSIONS AS REGARDS WATER SUPPLY

As regards the landings at Helles and Anzac in April, 1915, and the subsequent operations up to the end of July, we consider that the water arrangements at Helles were satisfactory, but that the daily allowance at Anzac was barely sufficient.

As regards the operations at Anzac in August, 1915, we find that, owing in some measure to the breakdown of a pumping engine and the collision of a vessel carrying 80,000 gallons of water with another vessel, there was a serious shortage of water, the allowance to each man being restricted to one pint a day. This may not have checked the action of the troops, but, as stated earlier, it precluded the sending of reserves when the attack was brought to a standstill.

As regards the landing at Suvla in August, 1915, we consider that:

(1) General Headquarters undertook the responsibility of arranging for the supply of sea-borne water and for the necessary equipment for its storage and distribution.

(2) Sufficient attention was not paid by Sir Frederick Stopford and his Administrative Staff to these arrangements, which should have been more thoroughly discussed between the Administrative Staff at General Headquarters and the Corps Administrative Staff before the landing. For the absence of such adequate consultation neither staff can be exonerated from responsibility.

(3) Besides the foregoing arrangements the questions which demanded special consideration on the part of Sir Frederick Stopford and his Administrative Staff were the action to be taken on the spot for the reception, storage and distribution of sea-borne water, including the provision of working parties to pump the water from the lighters; the expedients to be adopted in the event of delay in the landing of the pack mules, together with the filled water bags which they were to carry; and the instructions to be given for

the discovery and development of local sources of supply.

It appears to us that these questions were not sufficiently considered, and that Major-General Poett, Deputy Adjutant and Quartermaster-General of the IXth Corps, must be held to be primarily responsible for the lack of due consideration.

(4) The water shortage at Suvla abated after August 8th, but this fact does not excuse the want of organisation and prevision [foresight] which was apparent during the first two days, and which largely contributed to the inaction of the troops on the second day, and to the failure of the operations.

We are of the opinion that throughout the operations the Navy carried out their duties with regard to the supply of sea-borne water in an efficient manner, and were always ready to render any assistance in their power.

As regards the operations generally, and having in view the vital importance of water on the Gallipoli Peninsula, we consider that the question of water supply would have been more efficiently handled throughout if, following the analogy of food supply, a staff officer with the requisite qualifications had been appointed Director of Water Supply under the Quartermaster-General at General Headquarters, with a Deputy Director on the staff of each Corps Commander and an Assistant Director on the staff of each Divisional Commander.

FOOD

We think that, on the whole, the supply of food to the troops in Gallipoli was satisfactory.

MEDICAL

The provision for the evacuation of the wounded, especially in the matter of hospital ships, proved insufficient to meet the emergencies which actually arose. We think that, if the operations to be undertaken in landing on the peninsula had been considered before the expedition started and a general plan prepared, further provision of hospital ships might, and probably would, have been made.

We do not think that the Director of Medical Services, Surgeon-General Birrell, before leaving England had any opportunity of estimating the number of hospital ships required, as he did not know what operations were contemplated.

We think that the separation of the Administrative Staff, including the Deputy Adjutant-General and Director of Medical Services, from the rest of the Headquarters Staff during the time immediately preceding the landing was a mistake, and that it would have been better if the Director of Medical Services had been kept more fully informed of the operations which were proposed. The time was very short in which to make preparations, and we doubt if it was then possible to obtain a sufficient number of hospital ships to accommodate the casualties which actually occurred. If Surgeon-General Birrell had been able to discuss matters with the General Staff he might have seen the necessity of, and been able to obtain, a fuller supply of appliances and equipment for the transports.

We think, however, that it would have been well if, while in Egypt, where he was arranging for hospital accommodation on a large scale, he had made requisition for appliances such as would probably be required for even the less serious cases on the transports, such as bed pans, blankets, pillows, and clothing. We recognise, however, that at that time he was separated from General Headquarters, and therefore not possessed of adequate information as to the intended operations.

The scheme of evacuation drawn up by the Director of Medical Services was based on an estimate of casualties which was approximately correct, and would probably have worked satisfactorily if the anticipation of a rapid advance after the landing had been fulfilled. The failure of the scheme was mainly due to the fact that no substantial advance was effected, and that no hospitals could therefore be established on the land. This necessitated the immediate evacuation by sea of all casualties without any possibility of separating the serious cases from those of a slighter nature. The transports or black ships were therefore used for cases for which they were not intended, and for which they were not adequately staffed or equipped.

In these circumstances the greater part of the sufferings of the wounded in the first days after the landing seem to us to have been inevitable, but there appears to have been some want of organisation in the control of the boats and barges carrying wounded to the hospital ships and transports, which occasioned delay in their embarkation.

For the dislocation of the arrangements for evacuation, owing to the non-fulfilment of the expectations of the military authorities, the Director of Medical Services cannot be held responsible. He could not do otherwise than be guided by the views entertained by the Commander-in-Chief, and conveyed to the latter's subordinates in the operation orders and instructions for the landings issued by General Headquarters. It may indeed be contended that a prudent administrator, even though assured by a superior military authority of the probability of success, would do well not to leave out of account the possibility of failure; but to be prepared alike for either contingency demands a flexibility of organisation and an adaptability of resources, which in war are seldom attainable.

After the first two or three weeks, until the heavy fighting in August, there was an improvement in the condition of the transports, though some of them continued to be unsatisfactory. The transports required close supervision, which was, however, much hampered by the want of means of communication between the several ships and between the ships and shore.

The scheme for the evacuation of the wounded in the August operations was based upon an approximately correct estimate of casualties, and the supply of hospital ships was much larger than at the first landing. On the whole, this scheme worked well, though again there were cases in which the transports were not satisfactory and the organisation for transferring the wounded to the ships was imperfect.

After the middle of May the evacuation was made more difficult by the presence of enemy submarines. The transports were then unable to come to the beaches, the wounded being conveyed to them on trawlers and mine-sweepers, some of which were not suitable for their accommodation.

The field ambulances and clearing-stations were, on the whole, efficient, considering the great difficulties under which the work in them had to be done.

The executive work of the medical officers and staff of the Royal Army Medical Corps and the Dominion Forces, and of the physicians and surgeons who placed their services at the disposal of the War Office, was performed with great energy, courage, and skill under very trying conditions.

The supply of medicines and other medical requisites was, on the whole, adequate, though at times there was a shortage of some drugs at some places. The food also was on the whole satisfactory, but at times it was not possible to give the sick and wounded all the variety of food which was desired, and at times the supply of water was insufficient.

The difficulties under which the evacuation of the wounded was carried out, especially in the early part of the operations, were exceptional and not easily surmountable. We think that in some cases there was a want of organisation and supervision. The Director of Medical Services, Surgeon-General Birrell, did his best; we are of the opinion, however, that he was not equal to the task of grappling with the exceptional conditions which arose.

Great help was given by the naval surgeons on the transports as well as on the trawlers and sweepers, and they were always ready to do everything in their power. It was not, however, possible to employ them on the transports during their voyage to Alexandria or Malta, as they could not leave their ships for an indefinite time. The naval officers concerned in the evacuation of the wounded gave every assistance and rendered excellent service.

We have pleasure in recording our obligations to the Foreign Office, the Admiralty, the War Office, and the secretarial staff of the Committee of Imperial Defence, who have given us full information and every assistance in their power.

Finally we wish to express our high appreciation of the services rendered by our Secretary, Sir Grimwood Mears, to whom we are greatly indebted for the ability, tact, and industry which he has displayed throughout the course of the enquiry.

W. PICKFORD
NICHOLSON
W. H. MAY
GRIMWOOD MEARS   THOMAS MACKENZIE
Secretary   STEPHEN L. GWYNN
December 4th 1917   WALTER ROCHE

SUPPLEMENTARY REPORT
BY
THE HONOURABLE SIR THOMAS
MACKENZIE, KCMG

It is to be regretted that, for diplomatic reasons, a full
report of the evidence cannot be given to the public,
as the narrative must necessarily be inadequate. For
this reason, although I am substantially in agreement
with the findings of the Commission, I desire to supplement some of the conclusions reached by my

colleagues, and in addition I hold stronger views upon certain of the findings which I feel it my duty to put forward.

PREPARATIONS FOR THE CAMPAIGN

In my opinion, which I express with all deference, the forcing of the Dardanelles was a practicable proposition had the authorities approached the problem with a recognition of the nature and extent of the difficulties which confronted them, and made adequate provision and exhibited the necessary strength of purpose to carry the operations through to the desired end. History has demonstrated, and expert opinion supported, the view that a combined naval and military attack would ultimately offer the only chance of a favourable issue. The authorities should, I consider, have launched this combined attack only after thorough preparation, and I regard the preliminary bombardment of the outer forts on November 3rd, 1914—ordered by the Admiralty without consultation with the War Council—as an almost irreparable mistake. Its effect was to draw the attention of the Turks to the possibility of an attack in force on the peninsula, and there is no doubt it prompted them to make good use of the time which intervened between the November bombardment and the military landing on April 25th, 1915, in the way of improving their defences, etc.

Regarding the conduct of the military operations as a whole, it will be asked: "Was Sir Ian Hamilton the right man to command the expedition?" This question, in my opinion, we shall never be able to answer because he was hurriedly despatched, imperfectly instructed, and inadequately provided with men, artillery and munitions. Later on the deficiency in men was rectified, but although Lord Kitchener had said this was a young man's war, some generals were sent out to Sir Ian Hamilton who were unequal to the task. In this connection, let us glance for a moment at the methods of the War Office. General Sir James Wolfe Murray was the Chief of the Imperial General Staff. He was also a member of the War Council, and though he attended their meetings he expressed no opinions and tendered no advice, nor did he clearly understand that a decision was arrived at on January 13th to prepare for a naval attack on the Dardanelles in February.

Questioned later on as to whether it was not his duty, when the amphibious attack was decided on, to instruct the General Staff as to the preparation of plans, he admitted that under ordinary circumstances it was; and when asked to account for not doing so, he said in effect that he was overshadowed by Lord Kitchener.

Such a state of affairs at Headquarters did not presage a favourable inauguration or effective prosecution of the campaign, and the following statement of the position appears to me to be unassailable:

The Cabinet, having determined upon amphibious operations against Constantinople, necessarily left the preparations for and conduct of the military attack to the War Department. That system seems to be at fault which permitted:

(*a*) The outbreak of war to find the Imperial General Staff unprepared for operations against the Dardanelles and the Bosphorus—always of vital strategic interest for the British Empire in the East.

(*b*) The General Staff to remain inactive in that respect after August 4th, 1914.

(*c*) The General Staff to allow Sir Ian Hamilton to proceed to the Mediterranean without either a worked-out plan of attack or such primary requirements as verified or complete maps of the peninsula.

(*d*) The General Staff, notwithstanding their knowledge of the difficulties and lack of preparation, to silently acquiesce in this state of affairs.

To this breakdown of the War Office system on the testing ground of war may, in my opinion, be traced some of the vital factors of the Gallipoli disaster.

THE ATTACK AT SUVLA

The brief period from August 6th to 10th was, to my mind, the vital time in the history of the later Dardanelles operations, for on the wise and determined use of those few days depended the success or failure of the campaign. The objective was the range of hills controlling the Straits and the Narrows, the highest point of which was about 1,000 feet, three miles distant from the disembarkation point, the first two miles being easy, open country, the last mile rough and scrub-covered. Few Turks were then in the locality—estimates varied from 2,000 to 4,000—and prompt, decisive action was absolutely essential.

By daylight on August 7th General Stopford had landed over 13,000 men, and by the evening of that day 26,750 men. But the golden opportunity was thrown away by him and some of his officers, and the necessary swift advance—which military and naval witnesses thought quite possible—was not delivered, so that the Turks had time to bring up their reinforcements.

During the first four days, but mainly on the 9th and 10th August, General Stopford suffered 400 officer casualties and about 8,000 men killed and wounded. The failure at Suvla he attributes, not to the initial opposition of the Turks, but largely to the lack of water. He maintains that he relied on arrangements made by General Headquarters for the supply of water; but while that might have relieved him of the administrative work, it did not, to my mind, free him from the responsibility of seeing that the arrangements were carried out, and there is no doubt that the responsibility of distributing the water to his troops, if not of having it landed, rested with General Stopford and his subordinates. Nevertheless, until August 8th he took no active personal interest in this all important question.

Captain Carver, of the Royal Navy, did his best to encourage prompt action, but this was regarded by the military as undue interference, and he was withdrawn. No one seems to have been immediately answerable for supplying water, though undoubtedly General Poett's duties included its distribution. Except for General Sitwell's men, the troops were suffering severely from thirst, which impeded their operations. At the same time a barge of water was lying stranded within 100 yards of the beach, and the maps, captured from the Turks, showed that there were wells and springs within a quarter of a mile. We have General de Lisle's statement that:

> There were wells within a quarter of mile of the shore, which I had opened out. On the hill Kiretch Tepe Sirt there were two wells 400 feet higher than the sea, but on this side, between Kiretch Tepe Sirt and the Salt Lake, there were as many wells as you liked to dig.

Colonel Aspinall, too, states that he saw "a tremendous lot of water trickling down from the cliffs," and other witnesses declare that water was to be found. Yet General Poett neither made an attempt to procure water from the barge, nor to institute any search for water ashore. When questioned as to why he took no action, he disclaimed responsibility, contending that it was the duty of the Navy to get the water ashore, and of the Divisional Commanders to find it on land.

It is true that Sir Ian Hamilton cabled to General Stopford on the evening of August 7th–8th an appreciation of his work, but, as he afterwards explained, this cable was despatched before he visited Suvla, and when he was under the impression that everything was going well in connection with the operations.

OPERATIONS AT HELLES

In reference to Helles, attention should, I think, be directed to the evidence of some of the witnesses as to the frittering away of life through frontal attacks repeatedly carried out by General Hunter-Weston, in spite, it is alleged, of the absence of adequate artillery preparation and the lack of promise of substantial results. Lord Nicholson questioned Lieutenant-Colonel Wilson upon this matter, saying, "I suggest that in order to evade, so to speak, the necessity for an adequate artillery preparation, or the provision of artillery and ammunition, lives had to be sacrificed."

Colonel Wilson answered, "Yes."

Lord Nicholson continued, "In order to make good the deficiency of artillery and ammunition—that is the upshot of it?"

Colonel Wilson replied, "Yes, lives had to be sacrificed."

Lord Nicholson asked, "And almost with futility?"

"Yes, that is what I mean," said Colonel Wilson.

General Cox, too, considered that these frontal attacks fulfilled no useful function whatever, as at Helles the situation was hopeless tactically; but in reply to this, General Hunter-Weston stated that such attacks as were made were made for some reason which may not have been known to General Cox.

General Sir Ian Hamilton admitted to Lord Nicholson that lives were used instead of shells. He said:

> The vital thing was to make good, and to make good we ought to have had ample artillery, especially howitzers. We had not, and there was nothing for it but to try and get on, as you say, by a sacrifice of human life.

This matter is so serious that it seems to me to call for further enquiry, and this I recommend should be carried out by military experts.

EVIDENCE OF WITNESSES

With reference to the evidence tendered, whilst undoubtedly it was, in many respects, full and complete, yet one felt that some of the officers called as witnesses could have disclosed a great deal more than they did. Probably their reticence arose from a sense of loyalty to the Service and a disinclination to say anything against their comrades. As a consequence of this and the natural desire of the Commission to give those chiefly concerned the benefit of any doubt, some of the conclusions arrived at may be somewhat different from what they otherwise might have been.

TREATMENT OF WOUNDED

Until August, 1915, the arrangements for dealing with the transport of the wounded were in a very unsatisfactory state, and, indeed, the medical side of the campaign does not seem to have ever been thoroughly thought out. The treatment of the wounded ashore on the peninsula appears to have been as satisfactory as circumstances would permit, but in the transport of men to the ships and overseas many of the complaints were justifiable. The Medical Authorities contend that from the information supplied by the military commanders, they expected the Turks would be driven back and room would be made for establishing hospitals ashore. This, however, presupposed success, but better provision ought also to have been made for the contingency of failure.

A great strain was imposed on the arrangements—hospital ships were insufficient, and troop ships had to be rapidly converted into carriers and ambulance vessels; during the early days of the campaign undoubtedly a great deal of acute suffering resulted to the wounded from this cause. The extemporised [hastily prepared] hospital ships were insufficiently staffed, and there were not nearly enough medical officers of junior ranks, or female nurses, to attend to the patients. Although the medical personnel did their utmost, we hear of cases where men had to shift for themselves [manage] as best they could, and in fact some were left during the voyage to Alexandria in their first field dressings. General Maxwell testified that on some of the black ships the wounded were exposed to the sun and heat, with nothing to eat or drink, for 60 or 70 hours. Sir Frederick Treves gave evidence as to the absence of arrangements for the despatch of hospital ships, and the want of decision as to their destination.

There was also a general shortage of pillows, mattresses, fresh clothing, etc., and in some instances medical supplies and appliances were sadly lacking. In addition, the sanitary arrangements on the converted trawlers were lamentably deficient: the almost entire absence of such conveniences as bed pans, for instance, reduced the wounded to a deplorable condition.

That the medical arrangements must have been lamentably inadequate and the organisation seriously defective is confirmed by the fact that Surgeon-General Howse, VC, was impelled to give the following matured opinion:

> That he personally would recommend his
> Government, when this war is over, under no
> conceivable conditions to trust to the medical
> arrangements that may be made by the Imperial
> Authorities for the care of the Australian sick and
> wounded.

This is doubtless a strongly expressed view, and I think it is beyond question that a great improvement has been brought about since that time; but it is impossible to hold Surgeon-General Birrell free from a great deal of the responsibility for the serious condition of affairs to which Surgeon-General Howse and other witnesses drew attention.

THE *SATURNIA* CASE

Then we have the terrible story of the *Saturnia*— a most extraordinary indication of the absence of organisation. Father Barry first drew attention to the fact that 800 wounded men had been placed on that vessel, and the conditions which he brought to light as existing for a time, approximate to some of the revelations in connection with the Mesopotamian Medical Service. As the evidence stands I am unable to accept Colonel Maher's statement, sent by cable to the Committee, as giving an accurate description of the circumstances surrounding the case. I believe that Admiral Keyes, Fleet-Surgeon Levick, and Major Purchas gave the Commission the correct account of the conditions prevailing, and I concur in the suggestion that this matter should be further investigated. In this connection I should like to refer to the excellent work done by Fleet-Surgeon Levick and Major Purchas, and to the straightforward manner in which the evidence of all these officers was tendered.

THE WORK OF THE ARMY

Coming now to the work of the troops, I endorse the Majority Report that the men fought bravely and often heroically; and although there were certain phases of the conduct of the operations which led to misfortune and entailed great suffering, it is gratifying to know that there were in the Army on the peninsula men whose actions have not been surpassed by any deeds performed by the British Army. This applies to officers, NCOs and men. In my opinion, the outstanding figure in the campaign is General Birdwood, although many approached him in the excellence of their work, and shared with him in patient endurance the long and trying period of the Gallipoli operations. I should like to draw attention to the concluding work of General Birdwood and of those serving under him, in connection with the evacuation.

The opinion of experts who had studied the situation was that the evacuation might cost anything from 20 to 40 per cent in personnel and *matériel* [equipment]. The total number of the force evacuated was 125,000 men, and the whole operation was successfully carried out without the loss of a single life, and with only three men wounded—an achievement surely unsurpassed in the annals of history.

CONCLUSION

The Dardanelles Campaign with all its distressing circumstances and disappointments is now past history, and, without doubt, under the vigorous direction of Sir William Robertson, the haphazard, uncertain methods have largely disappeared and a good deal of the inefficiency which formerly prevailed has been swept away. If, however, the result of our investigations should assist in the bringing about of such an improvement in organisation and management as will render impossible a recurrence of events as sad as those with which we have had to deal, the work of the Commission will not have been in vain.

THOS. MACKENZIE

Other titles in the series

Lord Kitchener and Winston Churchill: The Dardanelles Commission Part I, 1914–15

"The naval attack on the Narrows was never resumed. It is difficult to understand why the War Council did not meet between 19th March and 14th May. The failure of the naval attack showed the necessity of abandoning the plan of forcing the passage of the Dardanelles by purely naval operation. The War Council should then have met and considered the future policy to be pursued."

Backdrop
The Dardanelles formed part of the main southern shipping route to Russia, and was of great military and strategic importance. However, it had long been recognised by the British naval and military authorities that any attack on the Dardanelles would be an operation fraught with great difficulties.

The Book
During the early stages of World War I, Russia made a plea to her allies to make a demonstration against the Turks. So attractive was the prize of the Dardanelles to the British generals, notably Lord Kitchener, that this ill-fated campaign was launched. Just how powerful an influence Kitchener was to exert over the War Council, and just how ill-prepared the Allies were to conduct such an attack, are revealed in dramatic detail in the report of this Commission.

The book covers the first part of the Commission's report. It deals with the origin, inception and conduct of operations in the Dardanelles from the beginning of the war in August 1914 until March 1915, when the idea of a purely naval attack was abandoned.

ISBN 0 11 702423 6   Price £6.99

British Battles of World War I, 1914–15

"The effect of these poisonous gases was so virulent as to render the whole of the line held by the French Division incapable of any action at all. It was at first impossible for anyone to realise what had actually happened. The smoke and fumes hid everything from sight, and hundreds of men were thrown into a comatose or dying condition, and within an hour the whole position had to be abandoned, together with about 50 guns."

Backdrop
On 4 August 1914, Britain declared war on Germany. Germany had already invaded Belgium and France and was progressing towards Paris.

The Book
These are the despatches from some of the battles of the first two years of World War I. They include action in northern France, Germany, Gallipoli, and even as far afield as the Cocos Islands in the Indian Ocean. They describe the events of battle, the tremendous courage, the huge losses, and the confusions and difficulties of war. These startling accounts, which were written by the generals at the front, were first published in the "London Gazette", the official newspaper of Parliament.

ISBN 0 11 702447 3   Price £6.99

Florence Nightingale and the Crimea, 1854–55

"By an oversight, no candles were included among the stores brought to the Crimea. Lamps and wicks were brought but not oil. These omissions were not supplied until after possession had been taken of Balaklava, and the purveyor had an opportunity of purchasing candles and oil from the shipping and the dealers in the town."

Backdrop

The British Army arrived in the Crimea in 1854, ill-equipped to fight a war in the depths of a Russian winter.

The Book

The hospital service for wounded soldiers during the Crimean War was very poor and became the subject of concern, not just in the army, but also in the press. "The Times" was publishing letters from the families of soldiers describing the appalling conditions. This embarrassed the government, but even more it irritated the army, which did not know how to cope with such open scrutiny of its activities.

The book is a collection of extracts from government papers published in 1855 and 1856. Their selection provides a snapshot of events at that time. In particular they focus on the terrible disaster that was the Charge of the Light Brigade, and the inadequate provisions that were made for the care of the sick and wounded. The documents relating to the hospitals at Scutari include evidence from Florence Nightingale herself.

ISBN 0 11 702425 2   Price £6.99

The Russian Revolution, 1917

"It is the general opinion in Ekaterinburg that the Empress, her son, and four daughters were not murdered, but were despatched on the 17th July to the north or the west. The story that they were burnt in a house seems to be an exaggeration of the fact that in a wood outside the town was found a heap of ashes, apparently the result of burning a considerable amount of clothing. At the bottom of the ashes was a diamond, and, as one of the Grand Duchesses is said to have sewn a diamond into the lining of her cloak, it is supposed that the clothes of the Imperial family were burnt there."

Backdrop

By November 1917 Russia had lost more than twenty million people in the war. Lenin's Bolshevik party had overthrown the Tsar and had called for an end to all capitalist governments.

The Book

Government files contain a number of detailed documents describing the nature of the Bolshevik Revolution and the government of Lenin, which was observed to be not only abhorrent but also menacing because of the international implications. The book is compiled from two of these files, one of which describes the events leading up to the revolution and how the Bolsheviks came to power in October 1917. The other contains a series of eye-witness accounts of the frightening days of the Bolshevik regime from the summer of 1918 to April 1919.

ISBN 0 11 702424 4   Price £6.99

UFOs in the House of Lords, 1979

"Is it not time that Her Majesty's Government informed our people of what they know about UFOs? The UFOs have been coming in increasing numbers for 30 years since the war, and I think it is time our people were told the truth. We have not been invaded from outer space. Most incidents have not been hostile. Indeed it is us, the earthlings, who have fired on them. . . . Whatever the truth is, I am sure that an informed public is a prepared one. Another thing: it is on record that both sighting and landing reports are increasing all the time. Just suppose the 'ufonauts' decided to make mass landings tomorrow in this country—there could well be panic here, because our people have not been prepared."

Backdrop

The winter of 1978/79 in Britain was a time of strikes and unrest. It became known as the "winter of discontent". Yet it seems that the House of Lords had other more important things to discuss.

The Book

The book is the transcript of a debate in the House of Lords which took place in February 1979. Their Lordships debated the need for an international initiative in response to the problem of Unidentified Flying Objects. There were several notable speeches from noble lords and distinguished prelates.

ISBN 0 11 702413 9   Price £6.99

D Day to VE Day: General Eisenhower's Report, 1944–45

"During the spring of 1945, as the sky grew darker over Germany, the Nazi leaders had struggled desperately, by every means in their power, to whip their people into a last supreme effort to stave off defeat, hoping against hope that it would be possible, if only they could hold out long enough, to save the day by dividing the Allies. Blinded as they were by their own terror and hatred of 'Bolshevism', they were incapable of understanding the strength of the bond of common interest existing between Britain, the United States and the Soviet Union."

Backdrop

In 1944 the Allies were poised to launch an attack against Hitler's German war machine. The planning and timing were crucial. In February, General Eisenhower was appointed Supreme Commander of the Allied Operations in Europe.

The Book

The book is Dwight D. Eisenhower's personal account of the Allied invasion of Europe, from the preparations for the D-Day landings in Normandy, France, to the final assault across Germany. He presents a story of a far more arduous struggle than is commonly portrayed against an enemy whose tenacity he admired and whose skills he feared. It is a tactical account of his understanding of enemy manoeuvres, and his attempts to counter their actions. The formality of the report is coloured by many personal touches, and the reader senses Eisenhower's growing determination to complete the task. Hindsight would have had the general take more notice of Russian activity, but that this was not obvious to him is one of the fascinations of such a contemporary document.

ISBN 0 11 702451 1   Price £6.99

The Irish Uprising, 1914–21: Papers from the British Parliamentary Archive

"Captain Bowen-Colthurst adopted the extraordinary, and indeed almost meaningless, course of taking Mr Sheehy Skeffington with him as a 'hostage'. He had no right to take Mr Sheehy Skeffington out of the custody of the guard for this or any other purpose, and he asked no one's leave to do so. Before they left the barracks Mr Sheehy Skeffington's hands were tied behind his back and Captain Bowen-Colthurst called upon him to say his prayers. Upon Mr Sheehy Skeffington refusing to do so Captain Bowen-Colthurst ordered the men of his party to take their hats off and himself uttered a prayer, the words of it being: 'O Lord God, if it shall please thee to take away the life of this man forgive him for Christ's sake.'"

Backdrop
In 1914 it was still the case that the whole of Ireland was part of Great Britain, under the dominion of the King, and Irish constituencies were represented in the British Parliament.

The Book
This book contains five remarkable documents published by the British Government between 1914 and 1921, relating to the events leading up to the partition of Ireland in 1921. In the first, a report is made into the shooting of civilians following a landing of arms at Howth outside Dublin. The second is of the papers discovered relating to the activities of Sinn Fein and particularly of Sir Roger Casement. The third is the government inquiry into the Easter Rising of 1916. The fourth describes the treatment of three journalists by the British Army shortly after the uprising, and the last is an exchange of correspondence between Eamon de Valera and David Lloyd George prior to the Anglo–Irish Treaty of 1921.

ISBN 0 11 702415 5   Price £6.99